ISBN: 9781676270928

LEGAL NOTICE

Ellen Frazier's 5 Step Checklist to a Hassle Free Home Buying Process

Step 1: Before you start your search for a home, meet with a mortgage loan officer and make an application for financing. Doing this up front will allow you to know how much home you can afford, the types of loans available as well as approximate monthly payments and closing cost.

By securing a complete pre-approval, you will make your house hunting more enjoyable.

Step 2: Make a list of what you are looking for in a house. You will want to consider location, type of home and the amenities the house offers. For example, do you want a home with a yard or would you prefer a condo?

Step 3: Select a Real Estate Agent to represent you. A good agent will listen to what you want in a home, and then they will do the research to find you the perfect match. Additionally, they will work to negotiate the best deal for your family.

Step 4: Tour homes that your agent locates and make your final decision. Be sure to contact your loan officer before making the offer on the home you select. Your loan officer will be able to give you accurate information on the closing cost and payments for the home you want to buy.

Step 5: Your agent will help you negotiate the offer and inspections. At the same time your lender will process your mortgage. After the appraisal, inspections and final underwriting, you will close on your home.

When you prepare in advance by hiring a seasoned professional, you will have a fun, enjoyable and simple home buying experience.

About Ellen Frazier

Ellen Frazier studied Art and Design at the University of North Carolina in Greensboro. She managed a ceramic tile and natural stone distributorship which led to her association with the National Association of Homebuilders. Her participation working with mortgage lenders as the Associate Member Committee Chair of that organization opened the doors for her venture into the mortgage business with Bank of America in Winston-Salem, North Carolina in 2004. Her experience there was a journey in compassion and in establishing a deeper understanding of peoples' dreams of homeownership. Making that very American dream a reality for Veterans and hardworking customers who aspired to that dream was her biggest joy and the key to her success. Ellen's promotion to management found her relocating to coastal South Carolina where she thrived and gained valuable experience with a wider variety of clients. In 2010 she joined forces with Wells Fargo where she managed a large team of top producing originators throughout the Lowcountry. Ellen has served since 2012 as a Director with the Mortgage Lenders Association of Greater Charleston. Ellen's continuous dedication to philanthropic efforts led her to a new, nationally successful organization. Early in 2017 she found and joined Movement Mortgage. You might have seen Ellen on the cover of Mount Pleasant Magazine's, Women in Real Estate Edition announcing her decision to join Movement Mortgage. When she joined the Movement organization Ellen knew she had found something special. The Movement Foundation's philanthropic efforts immediately grabbed her attention and her heart. This encouraged her to make a switch. Movement hosts an enormously wide variety of activities and endeavors. They partner in local markets to *give back* to the communities that they serve. Working both nationally and globally, Movement's Goals and Mission expanded Ellen's ideas of the possibilities for her to serve an even wider market of underserved people. You may find Ellen in West Ashley working with realtor partners and nonprofits alike, carrying out the mission of Movement Mortgage which is; "We exist to Love and Value People by leading a movement of change in our industry, in corporate cultures, and in communities."

Contact Ellen at 336-480-7383 or visit her online at www.ellenfrazier.com

Table of Contents

4 - Playing The Housing Market: Buying vs. Renting A Home

5 - Home Inspections

6 - Financing Your First Home

Preface

Before I write anything else, I want to say thank you for taking the time and picking up my book to read. While reading a book about real estate and mortgage financing isn't the most exciting topic in the world, it is an important one.

One of the things that you may notice is that there isn't any hyper local real estate information because as soon as I put it into print, things could change. The goal of this book is to give you a primer so you can become more educated about the process.

If you would like more information about a certain area of Charleston or the Tri-County area, please give me a call and I will give you a list of professional realtors that can answer your questions.

While I would love to help you with your mortgage lending, even if I don't get the opportunity, I hope you get value from my book and find your dream home. If I can help you in any way, please don't hesitate to reach out to me.

Ellen Frazier
336-480-7383

1
Overview

If you are currently living in an apartment or renting a house, you may be thinking about buying a home of your own for yourself and your family. This can be an exciting time. Looking at properties, deciding whether to buy a home or build a new one, and finding financing will take up a lot of your time.

There will be a long list of things you will need to do before you buy a home. This list includes:

- Finding the right neighborhood
- Finding a home that is big enough
- Finding the features you are looking for
- Choosing the right size yard
- Choosing a realtor
- Understanding the housing market
- The ins and outs of home inspection
- Financing
- Making an offer, and
- Reading contracts

This list does not include all of the decorating, home improvement, and other decisions you will have to make once you have purchased the home.

If you are a first time home buyer, you will be nervous about finding the right home, investing money on a down payment, and being approved for financing. Once you have found a home, it will usually take between two or three months before you will be able to move in. In the meantime, you should plan the following:

- Moving arrangements
- Home inspections
- Yard sales
- Budgeting for paint and other supplies
- Taking time off from work, and
- Finding a lawyer if necessary

Proper planning will help you transition into your new home much easier than if you wait until the last minute to deal with these details. If you are planning on moving yourself, you should find a few friends or family members that will be willing to help as soon as possible.

New Homes vs. Older Homes

Another decision you will have to make is whether to buy a new home or look for an older one. Most first time home buyers usually buy an older home, but this should not deter you from visiting a few builders to see what they are charging for the size of the home you are looking for.

Older homes may cost less, but they can be riddled with problems. In this book, you will learn what to look for when viewing a home, what to include in your purchase offer, and what to expect from a home inspection. There are many older homes that will need only minor repairs.

Which Home to Choose?

After you have looked into all of your options, you will be wondering which home to choose. There are many ways to find the home that is right for you. When looking at homes, you should keep these criteria in mind:

- Size
- Price
- Neighborhood
- Mortgage payments
- Repairs, and
- Additional features

While this is a short list, throughout this book you will learn other ways to find your dream home. In the end you will just know when you have found the right home.

Moving into your first home will be an experience you will never forget. You should be excited as this is a little piece of the world that is just yours. Whether this is the home you will live in for a long time or just for a short time, buying a home will give you a sense of pride and of purpose. Not only will you have a mortgage to pay, you will also be responsible for making the home your own. When thinking about purchasing as home, you should begin saving your money for closing costs, repairs, and decorating materials.

One of the more rewarding moments will be when you get the keys to your new home and you begin making it your own with a little paint, furniture, and personal style.

2
Location, Location, Location

Choosing where to live is almost as important as the type of home you want to live in. While this is a very personal decision, there are pros and cons to every neighborhood. But wherever you want to live, you will have to know where the highways are located, grocery stores, schools, and how far from work you will be. Buying a home means more than the structure you will be living in. It is also the community and the accessibility to places and events that mean the most to you and your family.

Finding the Right Neighborhood

How will you know you have found the right neighborhood? There are many ways to tell:

- You may feel a sense of calm
- The neighborhood may remind you of a happy memory
- You will be close to places you frequent often
- The neighborhood aesthetics are pleasing, or
- The rest of your family is pleased

You may feel one emotion or five when you turn the corner onto the street where you want to live. This will be an exciting time, especially if you have been searching for a home for the past few months.

When looking for the right location, you should consider the following:

- How clean is this neighborhood?
- Is this a high crime area?
- What is the average home value in the neighborhood?
- Are there community bylaws?
- What is the home close to?
- Is there garbage pickup?

While these questions may not include everything you are looking for when buying a home, they should be considered carefully as they will affect your life once you move into the home.

How Clean is this Neighborhood?

You should look at the neighborhood at different times during the day to see how those who live in the neighborhood take care of it. If there is a lot of trash on the ground, the yards are not kept up properly, or there are old signs posted on trees and telephone poles, then the neighborhood may not be for you.

If the neighborhood looks clean and you see people outside caring for their lawns, then you may have found a community of people who care about where they live. This is an important factor if you are planning on living in the neighborhood for many years. All too often people will buy homes only to discover that they live in a neighborhood where people do not have respect for their property or the property of others. This can make selling the home much more difficult in the future.

Is this a High Crime Area?

While all neighborhoods will experience some crime, you should consider buying a home in an area that has a high crime rate very carefully. While the home itself may be the right price for your budget, it may not be located in an area that is right for your well-being.

Drive by the neighborhood at nighttime to see if there is adequate street lighting, suspicious activity, or anything else that might cause you to use caution. Research the neighborhood and find out how the crime rate compares to other neighborhoods. If the crime rate is too high, then it may be best to look somewhere else.

What is the Average Home Value in the Neighborhood?

You can find this information out very easily by asking your realtor or by looking up this information at the county clerk's office or on their web site. You should be aware of the home values that are in your neighborhood for several reasons:

- Housing prices will vary depending on the neighborhood and region. You want to buy a home that you will be able to make a profit on when you decide to sell.
- You do not want to pay too much for a home.
- Giving a solid offer for the home means knowing what other homes that are similar in size are selling for.

Are there Community Bylaws or HOAs?

If you are looking at a home that is inside a community or homeowners association, you should be aware of yearly dues, rules about what can be in your yard (pool, lawn decorations, etc.) and any other rules that they may have.

Many people enjoy living in an HOA community because they feel safe and want to meet others in the neighborhood. HOAs usually have picnics and other events during the year where neighbors can meet each other. Some communities have pools, tennis courts, and other amenities. Traditionally, here in Spring Hill, you will find these to be townhouses or some people refer to them as condominiums. Unlike many larger cities, Spring Hill and the surrounding communities have very few HOAs that encompass single family homes.

What is the Home Close to?

When choosing a home, you will need to find the nearest grocery stores, schools, route to work, and other necessities that will make living in the neighborhood more convenient. Drive around the neighborhood to see what is around it. This will help make your decision to buy a home in a particular neighborhood much easier.

Is there Garbage Pickup?

While this may not seem like something you are interested in, when it comes to disposing of your trash, you may need to haul it to the dump yourself. Ask about trash pickup so that you can decide if this is something you really want to do on the weekend. This really is a question of living within the city limits or living in the country.

City Living vs. Country Living

Choosing the neighborhood you want to live in will also include deciding whether you want to live in the city, country or suburbs. Many people with families usually want to live in the suburbs because there is more room for children to grow, but is still close enough for parents to commute to work.

But there are advantages to city and country living as well. Those who live in the city will be close to work, restaurants, activities, and events. Those who live in the country, or as we say in the Spring Hill area, out in the country, may have a longer commute to work, but they will be able to enjoy the peace and quiet of having fewer people around them.

Whichever lifestyle you prefer, you should construct a pros and cons list that will give you a better idea of what to expect when looking for a home. Once you have looked at your list, you will have a better idea of which to choose. The following will get you started:

City Life
Pros
- Easy access to cultural events
- More options when eating out
- More grocery store and clothing store options
- Public transportation
- More people
- Choice of home styles, such as houses, condos, apartments, and
- Private and public schools

Cons
- Crime rates higher
- Pollution
- Higher housing costs
- Higher taxes
- Higher cost of living, and
- Not as much housing is available

Country Life
Pros
- More land available
- New homes available
- Less people, and
- Cost of living is lower

Cons
- Fewer schools to choose from
- Further from grocery stores and other stores
- Less people
- Not as many cultural events, and
- Longer commute to work

Suburban Living
Pros
- Close to city and country
- More land
- Cost of living is less expensive than city living
- Close to cultural events, and

- Community feeling

Cons
- More people in a smaller area
- Fewer schools to choose from, and
- Longer commute to work

When choosing the type of environment you would like to live in, the following may play a role in your final decision:

- Finances
- Schools
- Size of home desired
- Amount of land desired
- Taxes, and
- Length of your commute to work

You should check out both city and country living. While there will always be pros and cons, you should be able to find a home that will help you lead the type of lifestyle that is important to you and your family.

Making the Commute

You will have to count on the amount of traveling you will have to endure to and from your job when buying your first home. Unless you are relocating, you will have to find a neighborhood that is close enough to drive to or is accessible by public transportation. While some people enjoy sitting on a bus for an hour during the day, you may not want to use your time this way. Unfortunately, living in the suburbs or in the country may require you to make a longer commute.

If you want to remain relatively close to your job, you should not search further than a ten mile radius. Inform your real estate agent or drive ten miles in any direction and see what is out there. Many times there will be neighborhoods you have never heard of. You should find back roads a well as highway accessible roads that will make your commute easier.

You should also look for a home during different times of day in order to figure out the traffic patterns. If possible, live in an area that goes against normal traffic patterns. That way you will not be stuck in traffic going to work or when coming home.

Commuting to work can easily turn into a forty, fifty, or even an hour long drive depending on the time of day. While this may be inevitable, you should consider all of your options before purchasing a home.

Schools in the Area

If you have school age children, then you will want to find a home that is close to schools in the area. This goes for both public and private schools. If you find a neighborhood that you like, find out which school district it is located in. Not all school districts are alike and you will have to send your children to the school district your home is located in.

While your children do not have to walk to school, being relatively close to home will make it easier to pick them up, participate in after school events, and give them a sense of community.

If you are planning on living in the country, the nearest school could be very close to home or very far away, depending on where you move. The bus ride to and from school can be an hour or more. This could take time away from getting homework done or playing with friends. Be sure to weigh all of your options when choosing a home if you have children. Also, find out where the middle school and high schools are in the area. Eventually, your children will be attending these schools. Be prepared and find out everything you can about these schools as well.

Grocery Shopping and Other Necessities

While living in the country may seem peaceful, be prepared to do a lot more driving. The nearest grocery store or pharmacy may be thirty minutes or more. This is another factor you will have to consider when buying your first home. While small towns have centralized areas where the shops and grocery stores are located, unless you live in town, you will have to drive in order to get there.

Many people who live in the country will adjust their lives as well as their priorities. They may go to the grocery stores once every two weeks; they will not eat at restaurants as often, and will not go to the movies or other social events as often either. You will have to decide what is important to you.

Before buying a home, survey the town to see what is available. This will give you a good idea of what it would be like to live in the area. Spend a few days there if possible. This will save you from making a huge mistake later on.

If you are planning to stay in the city, you will have the advantages of public transportation, but you may still need a car for larger grocery shops.

While the city can be convenient in many ways, parking a car is not one of them. You will have to pay for garage parking in many instances, which will end up costing you more money than if you lived in the country. But, you will be able to get to these stores quickly and easily at any time during the day.

Other Location Considerations

Other location considerations include:
- Weather
- Road conditions
- Location of property in the neighborhood, and
- Room to grow

You should be thinking ahead in terms of the weather. If you are planning on living in the country, for example, you should pay attention to possible flooding, snow, and other weather that could affect you getting to work. If the road is a dirt road, you should ask if the county will clear the road an how often they will do so. This is another advantage of living in the city because you could always use public transportation if you do not want to drive.

The location of the property is also important. If the property is located at the bottom of a slope, you may have flooding issues after a rainstorm. Also, as your family grows, you many need more room. You should find property that can hold a home addition if necessary. Investigating in a home requires a great deal of thought and planning. Even if you do not have a family, you should find a home that will allow you to grow as your interests change.

3
Working With Realtors

If you are like many people, chances are good you looked around different neighborhoods, saw a few homes that were for sale, maybe visited an open house or two, and then felt stuck. What is the next step? Approach the homeowner? Visit the realtor?

Finding the right realtor when buying a home depends on what you are looking for in a home. You may have to visit several realtors before finding one that listens to your wants and needs. After all, you will probably be paying them a commission once you have found a home, so you should be comfortable working with them during the house hunting process.

Choosing a Realtor
There are a few ways to find a reliable realtor. For example, you can:

- Ask friends and family
- Ask other realtors
- Attend a few open houses and meet realtors
- Find ads online or in the newspaper
- Walk into a local office, or
- Look for local realtors in your neighborhood by paying attention to for sale signs in the neighborhood
- **Ask me for my list of personally endorsed agents – these are agents that I have interviewed, screened, and meet my high standards and my personal seal of endorsement!**

Asking plenty of questions before looking at houses may seem like a lot of work, but when you visit a realtor for the first time, you should think about questions that will help you get to know this person who is going to help you find your dream home. The five best questions to ask are:

1. Are you a certified realtor? (While all agents need to be licensed in all the states they are selling properties in, not all realtors belong to the National Association of Realtors.)
2. How long have you been in the real estate business?
3. Which neighborhoods are you the most familiar with?
4. How many homes do you have that will fit my needs?
5. What is your typical commission on a home in my price range?

Once you have asked these questions, you should be looking for honest and complete answers, good communication, and eye contact. These are questions that the realtor should have practice in answering and should not have to give you a standard 'salesperson' answer.

If you feel uncomfortable, then you are under no obligation to continue with this realtor unless they have some good property matches to show you. Normally, if a realtor does not have properties that fit what you are looking for, they will recommend you to another realtor in the group. This is also a good sign because it shows that the group is looking out for your interests and the interest of its employees.

You should also pay attention to:

- How well your realtor listens to what you are looking for
- How well they understand current real estate law
- How many other clients they seem to have
- How they speak to their coworkers
- How often they communicate with you on the phone or by email

In the end, you will have to be the judge of the real estate agent. If they know what you are talking about, can find out information you need quickly, and are willing to take time to listen to what you need, then you should work very well with them.

In some cases, you may be asked to sign an agreement that states you will only be working with a specific real estate agency or agent when looking for a home. You are under no obligation to sign this paperwork and you should only do so if you feel very comfortable.

While these agreements are not totally binding, it could make buying a home more difficult down the road. Only sign agreements if you feel very comfortable.

During your search for a real estate agent, you will find a variety of agents that will want to work with you. These include:

- Experienced agents
- New agents
- Pushy agents
- Absentee agents, and
- Hard working agents

While all real estate agents have different personalities, you will have to decide which one you will want to work with when looking for your new home.

Experienced Agents vs. New Agents

This is an age old debate that should be addressed. While an experienced agent may have sold more homes and earned more commissions, new agents can be just as helpful and need to get some sales under their belt, which may prompt them to work harder for you.

While you should ask about their experience, you should take into consideration other traits such as the ability to listen and the ability to show you homes in your price range. Experienced agents and new agents have been trained in similar fashion and only have their personalities to bring to the table.

There are experienced agents out there who will drag their feet because they are over confident or they are not as interested in their jobs as they once were. Experienced agents may know more about different neighborhoods, but some of them are not as proactive as they used to be.

You should not let inexperience deter you when looking for an agent. Many times new agents will work harder because they want to gain a reputation that they can use to build confidence in their future clients.

Pushy Agents

Unfortunately, you will meet real estate agents who will want to sell you more than you need. In an effort to earn larger commissions or sell those properties that are more difficult, many agents will try this tactic. This is where you will need to stand firm. You do not want to waste your time looking at homes that are beyond your price range unless you can find a way to lower the price.

While looking at possible homes is exciting, this will not last long as you will grow weary of spending all of your available time looking for a home. If an agent keeps showing you homes that are out of your price range, then you should consider finding another agent.

Absentee Agents

Absentee real estate agents are those agents who show you a few homes and then disappear for a few weeks. These agents may be overworked, may not be able to find a home in your price range or neighborhood, or have higher priced commissions to find. Whatever the reasons, this is unprofessional behavior and should be rectified immediately, especially if you need to find a home quickly.

If an agent does not have homes in your price range or neighborhood, they should recommend another agent in the group. Agencies never want to lose customers. If your agent does not do this, find a new one.

Even agents who are overworked have time to make a quick phone call. If you do not hear from your agent in a week after your last meeting, find another agent.

Hard Working Agents

These are the best agents to find when you are buying your first home. If you find an agent like this one, do not lose them. These are the agents that will follow every lead, pass your wants and needs to another agent, and try their best to find you a home. You should expect to see a handful of homes when working with an agent like this one.

Now that you know more about what to look for in a real estate agent, you should feel a little more comfortable about working with one. They can be an invaluable source of information when you want to know more about homes, neighborhoods, and other questions about the communities you are looking at.

When looking at homes with your real estate agent, you should ask questions about the home, the neighborhood, the city or town, and any other questions you need to know in order to make an informed decision. Part of your real estate agent's job is to research homes and neighborhoods so that they can answer questions that may come up.

Preparing to See Homes with Your Realtor-
Create a List

Once you have found a realtor you are comfortable with, you will want to make the most of your time when house hunting. Giving your realtor a list of what you are looking for will help narrow the search and save everyone some time. Your list should include:

- Your price range
- Number of bedrooms you want
- Number of bathrooms
- Size of property
- Basement (finished or unfinished)
- If you want a porch, patio, or balcony
- Central heat and air conditioning
- Garage
- Neighborhood, and
- Any other amenities you would like

Giving your real estate agent a list of your preferences will allow them to spend more time researching homes that fit the criteria. You should list these amenities from greatest to least important because no home is perfect and you will not get everything you want or need. Let your agent know that you are flexible, but that you really want to concentrate on certain items when looking for a home.

Viewing Homes
When looking at homes with your agent, be sure to ask any questions you may have. While these questions may seem small, they may be important to your happiness. Common questions people ask their agents are:

- How old is the home?
- How many owners has the home had?
- What kinds of renovations have been done to the home?
- How old is the plumbing?
- How old is the wiring?
- How low are the sellers willing to go?
- How old is the carpeting and flooring?
- How old are the windows?

While your agent may answer some of these questions before you ask them, you should ask any questions that may influence your decision to buy a home. If you do not want to put too much work into fixing up the home, you may want to buy a home that is ten years old or less.

If your agent does not know all the answers to your questions, they should be able to find out and will give you a call within a day or two.

Taking Pictures
One of the best ways to remember the homes you have seen is to bring your camera and take pictures. Get permission from the agent first before taking pictures of another person's home.

Many times, after looking at a few houses, you will forget how big the kitchen in home number two was in comparison with home number five. Having pictures will give you a better idea of the square footage and how much room you will have to work with.

Narrowing Down Your Choices
After a few weeks of viewing homes that fit what you are looking for, you should be close to finding a home that you will want to make a bid on. If you have other homes you would like to see or have changed your mind as to what you are looking for, you should tell your agent so that they can look for other homes.

Many times, if a person likes the neighborhood but not the home they were shown, they will want to see other homes in the neighborhood that are for sale. You should ask to see all of the homes available in a neighborhood that you like.

If you are still not finding a home that you like, you may need to change the neighborhoods you are looking it. While this can seem disappointing, your real estate agent will be happy to show you homes in different neighborhoods. Sometimes if you compare homes to one another, you will find redeeming qualities in a home you have already seen. Once you have found a home that you like, you should make an offer. Contact your agent as soon as you can so that they can draw up the paperwork, contact the seller's agent, and make an offer before another person does. Make an offer as soon as you can in order to avoid a bidding war.

Bidding can be long and drawn out in some cases. If you do not have the time to wait out a bid or if you cannot bid any higher, then you may be looking for another home to purchase. While this can set you back, you should try to stay positive and find a home that is right for you.

Your agent should be there to guide you along during this time. Ask all the questions you have before making an offer on a home.

Information Realtors Should Tell You

There is plenty of information that realtors can tell you about the homes you will be viewing. Things they should tell you include:

- The price of the home
- The age of the home
- Any renovations that have been done
- Any other issues with the home
- Property taxes
- Community dues
- Schools
- Neighborhood crime rates, and
- The median age of those who live in the neighborhood

Usually, if a realtor does not have the information you request on hand, they will be able to look it up once they are back in their office. You should be able to find out all the information you need to know in order to make an informed decision about buying a home. Realtors are required by law to give you information concerning repairs, damage, and the history of a home. This includes any incidents that have occurred inside the home such as criminal activity, fire, and other events.

You can also do a little research of your own by using the Internet, which has become a wonderful tool to use when searching for a home. You can research past events that have taken place in the neighborhood, the home itself, or the town where you want to live. Knowing a little history may prompt you to look elsewhere or make an offer.

Other information realtors can tell you include:

- Home owner price reduction (your realtor will talk with the seller's realtor once you have made an offer or want to make an offer to see how low the owners will go to sell the home
- Prices of other homes in the area that are comparable to the one you are looking into buying
- How quickly the owner wants or needs to sell their home
- How much you will have to pay in property taxes each year, on average
- Other taxes in the area

Your realtor is a person who should be well acquainted with the neighborhoods you are looking at when buying your first home. Don't be afraid to ask many questions.

Working with Seller's and Buyer's Agent

As a home-buyer, your real estate agent is considered the buyer's agent. While some people will forego hiring an agent at first when looking for a home in order to save money on commission costs, they will usually end up hiring an agent to:

- Handle negations with seller
- Do paperwork, and
- Survey neighborhoods

It is in your best interest to hire an agent in order to make buying a home a much easier and faster process.

Negotiations with Sellers

Most people who sell their homes are also working with an agent. This agent is known as a seller's agent. If you choose not to hire an agent, you will be dealing with a seller's agent who is looking out for the home-owner's interests, and not yours.

Sometimes, though, the seller's agent and the buyer's agent can be the same agent. This means that your agent is looking after the interests of everyone involved. This is a rare occurrence, and it is best to hire an real estate agent who can negotiate with other agents in order to get you the best deal on a home.

Negotiating with agents can take a week or more depending on how high you are willing to go and how low the owners are willing to go. This can become a complicated game once you introduce home inspectors. After an initial home inspection, if you feel there are repairs that should be made prior to the sale of the home, or if you want a price reduction because of the repairs you will have to make, you will have to negotiate with the owners to settle on a fair price. Without an agent, you will have to do all of this work yourself.

Paperwork

When buying a home, there is a lot of paperwork that must be completed before the closing. This paperwork can include:

- Offers
- Counter offers
- Home inspection reports
- Home appraisal reports, and
- Fixture lists (Items that come with the home and items you would like removed)

Filing the paperwork is not difficult, but it can take some time. Working with an agent will save you time and money when creating and sending out various paperwork.

Survey Neighborhoods

Another advantage to hiring an agent is that you will not have to do as much legwork in the beginning. You may have a few neighborhoods in mind, but you will be able to leave it up to your agent to find homes for sale and setting up appointments to see them.

This is another time save especially if you have to work during the week. Taking time from your busy day to call other agents and homeowners to set up appointments will distract you from your other daily duties.

More Reasons to Hire a Real Estate Agent

There are several other reasons to hire a real estate agent. These include:

Peace of Mind

The bottom line is that a buyer's agent is the best resource when it comes to finding and making an offer on a home. While a seller's agent will be able to tell you the basics about a home, they are working for the homeowner. They will not try to get you the lowest price for the home. If you enjoy negotiating, then working with the seller's agent might be for you. But, if you are like most people, hiring an agent to work on your side will make the entire process more enjoyable and worthwhile in the end.

Wealth of Knowledge

Your agent will be very knowledgeable about negotiating the right price for your new home. They will be able to help you decide where you want to live, and they will be able to guide you in buying or walking away from any property you are not sure about. This is why it is so important to talk with your agent and ask as many questions as you can before buying a home.

Confidence

If you are having doubts about purchasing the home you have made an offer on, then you should tell your agent right away so they can postpone the offer made and help you reexamine what it is you are looking for in a home. Many times the initial shock of being a homeowner can be overwhelming. Sometimes talking with your agent is enough to resolve your feelings. Other times, you may need to see a few more homes before making a decision. Your agent will be able to give you practical advice during this time.

4
Playing the Housing Market: Buying vs. Renting a Home

Now that you know more about finding a real estate agent, you should begin watching the housing market carefully in the weeks or months before buying your first home in order to get a feel for whether it is in your favor.

Watching the Housing Market

For the past year, the housing market has been favoring buyers. Soaring market values were short-lived as many people decided they just could not afford to live in certain areas because of the cost of housing. This has caused many sellers to lower their prices. While this sounds like good news for you, the housing market can be very fickle. Depending on where you want to live, you may end up having to pay a small fortune for the home of your dreams.

This is why watching the market, surveying neighborhoods, and finding a good agent will help you in your search.

While you should not become a slave to the housing market, you should keep the following in mind before buying your first home:

- The past market value of the home you are interested in buying
- How much house your budget can get you in different neighborhoods and towns
- Neighborhood value
- How much the home should increase over time, and
- Price reductions that may be available

Just because you buy a home for a great deal does not mean you will make a huge profit when it is time to sell it. The housing market will continue to change and since this is your first home, you may want to choose something you can pay off quickly and make a larger profit on in the future.

Also, remember that any improvements you make on the home will increase its overall value. Just don't spend too much money on improvements. Creating a home improvements budget and sticking with it will help you make those monthly mortgage payments and other payments that will be due.

One of the biggest mistakes that the first time homeowners can make is buying a home for a lot less than they budgeted and then making improvements that will end up costing more money in the end. If you can find a great deal on a home, use that extra money as a cushion in case you lose your job or are too ill to work. Owning a home is a big responsibility. Knowing how the market is moving and spending your money wisely will help when you are creating a budget, applying for a mortgage, and deciding how much to put down on a home.

Making the Most of the Housing Market

While you should be watching the housing market, there are other areas of interest you should be watching also, such as:

- National interest rates for mortgages
- Building rates in your area
- Number of foreclosures in your area, and
- Stock market and gasoline prices

National Interest Rates for Mortgages

Even though the housing market may be going your way does not mean that the interest rates you could be paying are. In the times when the housing market has taken a slump, interest rates tend to rise in order to retain the natural balance within the economy.

The interest rate you receive will depend on many factors, including:

- Other loans
- Current credit score
- Credit history
- Number of credit cards
- Yearly income
- Owed debts
- Current interest rates
- Type of lender
- Time of year, and
- Adjustable and fixed rate mortgage

If you see housing prices dropping, you may opt to buy a larger home than you would have if the prices had been higher a year ago. While you will be saving money on that end, you may be paying more each month because of the interest rate you received.

Building Rates in Your Area

If you notice the housing market has also caused the building of new homes in your area to decrease, then you may have to enter into a bidding war in order to buy your first home. When new home construction goes down, this can mean one of several things:

- The area is no longer popular
- The interest in buying a new home has diminished
- People can no longer afford to purchase new homes
- People are opting for older homes that are less expensive to heat and cool during the year

While that housing slump may bring a reduction of housing prices, you should consider making a bid soon after finding the home of your dreams because bidding wars will only end up costing you more money.

Number of Foreclosures in Your Area

When looking for a home, you should consider looking at homes that are under foreclosure. This can be for many reasons, but usually banks that hold the titles want to unload these homes quickly so that they do not lose more money than necessary. Many times auctions will be held or the home will be advertised as a foreclosure in the newspaper or online.

You should check out these homes because you may find exactly what you are looking for in a home.

Stock Market and Gasoline Prices

Even if you do not play the stock market game or own a car, you should still pay attention to these areas because they are usually what will dictate housing prices and the cost to heat and cool the home.

When the stock market is doing well, many people will spend their money freely, which will give way to higher housing prices. But, when gasoline prices go up, so will the price to heat and cool a home, which may make home buyers reconsider buying until prices fall again.

This could be a good time to buy a home if you are willing to pay a little more each month in utility costs.

The impact society can have on the housing market can be huge, and it can also have lasting effects. Buyer's markets are created when there are more homes available than buyers, while seller's market occurs when there are more people who want to purchase homes than there are for sale. These housing markets go back and forth due to issues mentioned above.

In the End

In the end, when you are ready to buy a home, you should make the decision based on what you can afford and how much money you can put down for your new home. Just because you find a home that has a huge price reduction and you are comfortable financially, does not mean you must buy that home.

Buy a home when you are ready. Many times, people will buy a home because it is cheaper in the long run than paying rent each month. The downside to home ownership is that you have to make your mortgage payments on time each month. Very few lenders will give you more time to come up with the money. If you miss even one payment, your home could be foreclosed upon. You will have no place to live and your credit score will suffer severely.

If you can afford to make the move into your new home now, you should not wait too long before making an offer. The housing market can change quickly and with competition out there, you may end up losing more money if you don't make an offer after seeing a home that you like.

Buying vs. Renting (Pros/Cons)

Even though in the long run, buying a home is more cost effective than renting a home because of the equity that will build up over time, many people are just not comfortable carrying the weight of paying for a home on their shoulders. Also, those who have to travel often for work may not want the day to day upkeep that owning a home requires.

There are plenty of pros and cons when it comes to buying a home versus renting a home. Since you are thinking about buying your first home, you should consider these pros and cons for several reasons. First, if you are currently renting a home, you may want to invest in property that you can later sell. Second, you will be responsible for repairs and maintenance for the home instead of being able to call your landlord or maintenance crew. The third reason you should weigh the pros and cons is if you are planning to move in the next few years. If the housing market is a buyer's market for now, you may have difficulty selling the home later on.

Buying a Home
Pros
- Investment property – value will hopefully only increase or remain the same
- Build equity that you can use later on
- You can improve upon your home any way you want
- You can decorate it to suit your needs
- No landlord or property management company
- Sense of stability
- Ability to live in a community, and
- You have something to sell later on

Cons
- You are responsible for all repair and maintenance costs
- Monthly payments for utilities and mortgage are more expensive
- Could take time to sell later on

Renting a Home
Pros
- You are not responsible for repairs and maintenance costs
- You are free to leave once the lease has expired
- In many cases, utilities are being paid by the landlord
- Many apartment buildings have some sort of security system
- Usually less expensive than paying a monthly mortgage
- Credit score is unaffected if rent cannot be paid on time

Cons
- Privacy issues
- May have to share washers and dryers
- Rent to be increased once lease expires
- Landlord may not fix items on time
- Cannot paint walls or add other features
- Deposit may be required
- May not allow pets
- Neighbors come and go

As you can see, there are many factors that you should consider when thinking about buying your first home.

But if you are ready financially and want to have your own space, you should find an agent and start looking. The average time that most people take to make an offer on a home once they start looking is two weeks. If you have not found a home within that time, you should either continue looking or rethink your decision. There is nothing wrong with waiting a few months until you are ready.

Rent to Own

Another option you may have is to buy the property you are currently renting or rent a property that also offers you the option to buy after a certain amount of time. This will give you a chance to see if you like living in the home and will give you time to get your finances in order.

Rent to own properties are usually older than other homes and have been rental properties for some time. This means that they may not be in great shape. If you are looking for a property that you don't mind repairing, then this option may be for you.

When looking for a rent to own property, you should ask the following questions:

- How old is the home?
- How many times has it been rented out?
- What is the mortgage payment on the home?
- What is the rent per month for the home?
- How long will I have to make my decision?
- What happens if I change my mind?

You should still sign the proper contracts stating that you are interested in buying the home after a given time period. This will protect your rights and the rights of the current homeowner.

New Homes

When you think of your first home, you may be thinking of a brand new home. If the housing market is favoring buyers at the moment, you may get a great deal from a builder that is developing a new housing community, or you may find a plot of land that is in an existing community. This can be a great alternative to buying an older home for many reasons:

- You will have a part in designing the home
- You will have new appliances and lighting fixtures
- You will have new carpeting and flooring
- You will be able to choose all of the fixtures, carpeting, and flooring

- You will be able to add a porch or a patio, and
- You will be able to place the home where you want it on your property.

A new home can be very exciting, but it can also be a lot of extra work. The first step in buying a new home is to find property. You should visit builders and real estate agents who will file all of the necessary paperwork, permits, and other items needed to build on the property. This can take a few weeks, so be sure to plan accordingly.

The next step is to design the home. This is the fun part where you will get to personalize your home to suit your needs.

Once you have been approved for a mortgage, the property has passed all of the land inspections, and the home has been designed, construction will begin. Depending on the time of year, you will have to wait about three months before you can move into your new home.

After construction is complete, you should complete a walkthrough of the home, check all of the fixtures, and have the home inspected before signing the final paperwork. Then the home is yours.

Many people hire a lawyer during the construction phase so that all of the paperwork has been filed and there are no problems during the walkthrough.

Buying a new home is just one more option you should consider when looking for your first home. Home construction can vary as there are a few ways to build a home, including pre-fab homes that will be built elsewhere and delivered to your property where they will be assembled. Look into all of your options before deciding on a home that is right for you and your budget.

Using the Housing Market to Your Advantage

By paying attention to the current housing trends and keeping a watchful eye on the homes in our area, you will be able to make an offer on a home that will be accepted. While the market is continually changing, it is a useful tool for those who are on a budget, who want to find a home that is large enough to suit their needs, and will be worth more when it is time to sell it.

When watching the housing market, consider the following:

- The number of homes that are in your area
- The number of days the homes have been on the market
- The price of a new home compared to those that are being sold by homeowners
- The price of renting vs. buying
- The number of homes that are in your price range
- The highest price you can pay when buying a home
- Interest rates in comparison to housing prices, and
- The time of year

Springtime is a good time to buy a home for several reasons:

- More people want to sell
- It is easier to make appointments to view homes
- Prices are usually lower
- People are more willing to reduce their asking price
- Income tax returns can help with a buyer's budget

There will be plenty of people who could not sell their homes in the fall or winter months and who are trying to sell before summertime. Homeowners that need to sell their homes before a certain time are more willing to reduce the price of their homes.

While you should consider looking at a home during any time of the year, you will find that many homes will be lower in the spring to attract buyers.

This is also the time when interest rates are re-evaluated and many lenders are willing to give loans to those whose credit is not the best. Take advantage of when interest rates are at their lowest even if it means accepting an adjustable rate mortgage. You will have the option of locking into a fixed rate at a later time.

While the housing market can change, the idea of selling one's home will not. Homeowners may choose to wait out the current housing market, but if they are eager to buy another home or move to a new place, their wait will be short-lived. Negotiate with homeowners until a fair price can be reached. This is the same practice during a seller's market as in a buyer's market. You may have to play the bidding game for a week or two, but in the end, it is the person who needs to make the transaction happen the most that will end up compromising the most.

5

Home Inspections

A home inspection will give you a chance to discover more about the home before you purchase it. In case there are serious problems with the foundation, mold issues, or underground leaks, you will be prepared to ask for repairs, a reduced price, or walk away from the property.

The Importance of Home Inspections

Finding a home does not mean that your investigative duties are over. Although most states do not have required inspections, your lender may require at the very least a pest inspection that will need to be conducted before they agree to approve your mortgage loan. If there are termites or other insects, the homeowners will have to take care of the problem before they sell the home.

But what about full home inspections? Are they worth it? In most cases, the answer is yes. Although you will have to pay for a home inspection, it may save you a lot of money in the long run.

A thorough home inspection will include checking the following:

- Electrical systems
- Heating and cooling systems
- Foundation
- Siding
- Structural elements
- Roof
- Insulation
- Doors and windows, and
- Plumbing

If you are buying a new or used home, it is best to have a home inspection before signing the final paperwork. Once the inspection report comes back, you will have the opportunity to ask the homeowners for a price reduction, go ahead and buy the home anyway, or ask the homeowners to make the necessary repairs.

You will have a varied reaction from homeowners. Many times, they will agree to lower the price a little.

When drawing up the initial offer for the purchase of the home, you should include a statement that allows you to withdraw your bid if any repairs are not taken care of or the price is not lowered due to the findings by the home inspector. If the contract does not include this, then you can still withdraw from the bid, but you may owe the agent commission fees.

Having a home inspection will give you peace of mind when you are buying a home. Since you will be taking out a mortgage, it is important to know what you will be buying, and the amount of money you will have to invest after purchasing the home. A home inspection will also help you make your final decision whether to purchase the home or to keep looking for another.

How to Find a Home Inspector
There are a few places to turn when looking for a home inspector:
- Your real estate agent
- References from friends and family
- The phone book, and
- Contractors

Ask around and see if you can get references of other homeowners that will give you a good report. Many home inspectors work freelance and only work certain days during the week. They are trained in home inspection and many are retired contractors, builders, electricians, and plumbers who know what they are looking for.

When you find a few home inspectors, give them a call and ask the following questions:
- How long have you been inspecting homes?
- How much do you charge per hour?
- What do you look for when inspecting a home?
- What types of reports should I expect?
- What days during the week are you available?
- Do you offer septic system inspections?
- What type of licensing do you have?

A thorough home inspection should take an inspector about three hours to complete. This will give you an idea of how much the inspection will cost.

Once you have asked these questions, find out if your lender has specific inspections that the home must pass before you will receive a home loan. If the inspector can complete these inspections along with the home inspection, then it is worth the time and money to have the inspector complete all the inspections on the same day.

The next step after choosing an inspector and finding out which inspections will be needed by your lender is to make sure the homeowners will be home for the inspection. Usually your agent will arrange a time for the inspector to perform the inspection.

It is up to you if you would like to be present for the inspection or not. Many times, the reports will be enough to give you a clear idea of what needs to be done. After the inspection is complete and the reports have been completed, it is up to the homeowners to either make the repairs necessary or lower their asking price.

If the repairs are minor and will not require too much money to repair, they will usually agree to make the repairs. If you would like to absorb the cost of the repairs, then you can offer to do so. You should receive this decision in writing so that there is no confusion during the final walkthrough before the closing. At the closing, you should have all of your paperwork, including the home inspection reports with you in case there is a discrepancy.

What to Expect from a Home Inspection
A home inspection can unearth many problems you did not notice during your visits to the home. Typical findings include:

- Crumbling foundation
- Structural damage to floors, walls and ceilings
- Water damage inside and outside the walls
- Termite damage
- Porch railings or posts in poor condition
- Heating and cooling systems need to be cleaned or do not work properly
- Roof needs repair
- Sinkholes
- Broken or leaking pipes

- Electrical wiring not functioning or broken
- Broken water fixtures or light fixtures
- Windows that do not open
- Uneven doorways
- Improper insulation
- Mold
- Water contamination
- Septic tank issues, or
- Hazardous chemicals

Most homes will only experience a few minor issues, but some older homes may have more problems than they are worth. The damage to the homes could cost you thousands of dollars if you are unaware of the damage prior to purchasing the home. While disclosure of some problems is mandatory, many homeowners do not even know that some of these problems exist until they try to sell their homes.

On the day of the inspection, you should expect to hear about some of the problems. You should be given a detailed report of the findings that will outline drastic problems and those that can be fixed easily.

Some lenders will not approve the home loan until the problems are fixed and another inspection is conducted.

Specific Places that Should be Inspected
When interviewing home inspectors, make sure to ask whether the following areas are inspected:

- Chimney and fireplace
- Attic and basement
- Crawl space
- Swimming pools, and
- Smoke detectors and appliances

These are important areas that can be very costly to repair once you have purchased the home. Many homeowners are willing to replace a chimney cap or remove mold from the basement. You should make sure that these areas are inspected prior to the closing. You should also inspect these areas during the final walkthrough.

Chimney and Fireplace
Inspectors should be looking for:

- Missing, broken, or intact chimney caps
- Mortar between chimneys is intact
- Metal chimneys are not bent or contain holes and have all screws in place
- Creosote – this is buildup caused from wood burning fireplaces, and is flammable if not removed

Attic, Basement, and Crawl Spaces
Home inspectors should be on the lookout for the following:

- Mold
- Fire damage
- Rotting beams
- Insulation
- Damage from water, and
- Damage from animals and pests

Swimming Pools
When looking at the swimming pool, the inspector should look at the following:

- Swimming pool plumbing, and
- Swimming pool shell

Smoke Detectors and Appliances

- Make sure they work
- No leaks
- Check for broken hoses or connections
- Broken door handles
- Inadequate wiring

Termite Inspection
A termite inspection is a separate inspection that will give you an idea of structural damage to the home that has been caused by termites and other pests. This inspection is required by most lenders before they will guarantee you the money to purchase the home.

Termite inspections are not covered under the standard fee of a home inspection, so you may have to pay for the inspection unless the homeowners are willing to do so.

The inspection should take about an hour and will entail the inspector looking underneath the siding, in basements, attics, and on the foundation of the home to see if there are termites present or if there are other insects such as ants, or fungus that are destroying the wood. The inspector will also conduct an inspection inside the home as well. Since termites can live in different weather conditions, you should have the inspection done even if you live in an area that has lower temperatures than other regions.

Termites can be removed using an insecticide that is specially designed to kill termites and their eggs, but the damage left behind can be immense. If the home has been infested for a long time, then it may be beyond repair.

You will then have to discuss a reduction in price, repairs being made to the property, or walking away altogether.

How Homeowners Will React

How the homeowner will react to the results of the home inspection could determine whether you continue pursuing the home or whether you let it go and find another one.

Homeowners have their own agenda when it comes to selling their home. These include:
- Buying another home
- Moving to another state
- Using the money to pay for family medical emergencies
- Retirement, or
- Making money on an investment property

This means that there are varying degrees as to what they are willing to pay for and what they are not willing to pay for. If the homeowner is not in a rush to sell, then they may contest the findings and refuse to repair certain items. If they need to make as much money as possible, they may agree to lower the price a little or make repairs that cost the least on the list.

You will have to make some tough decisions at this point. If the repairs will be needed on the home are required by the lender, you can:

- Try to find another lender
- Try to get the homeowners to pay for the repairs
- Pay for the repairs yourself, or
- Walk away from the home

Whichever decision you make, you will have to live with the consequences.

Homeowners know they are taking risks when selling older homes. But what about new homes? If your new home does not pass inspection, it is up to the builder to make the necessary repairs. You should make sure this is included in the contract before signing it.

If you are buying a home that the homeowners have already moved out of, you may be able to get the repairs paid for without having to be too pushy. If the homeowners are paying another mortgage, they are eager to sell and may opt to pay for the repairs upfront or give you a price reduction. This will depend on the circumstances. There is always a certain amount of luck that goes into buying a home.

Ways a Home Inspection Can Lower the Final Price

Even though you will have to spend money upfront for a home inspection, you may save more money than you anticipated once the results come back. This is especially true for older homes or new homes that were not built using the right materials or according to safety codes.

There are a few ways you will be able to negotiate a lower price on the home before signing the final contracts.

- **Ask homeowners to make repairs**
  This is the best way to save money on your new home. While you will not see a reduction in the final price of the home, you will not have to make as many repairs down the road. Also, you will not have to worry about the repairs once you have moved into the home.

  While all homeowners are different, you should be aware that many do not want to make repairs unless the home absolutely cannot be sold in the condition it is in because it will endanger the new owners. Even minor repairs may pose a problem for homeowners. You should be firm, but friendly when negotiating this part of the contract. If you do not want to make these repairs and you strongly feel that the repairs should be made by the homeowner, you can still walk away from the home and find another.

You should give the homeowners a week to think about making the repairs. Most homeowners will make their decision quickly because they want the sale to go through.

- **Ask homeowners for a price reduction**
  If the homeowners do not want to spend money on the repairs that you have requested, they may agree to drop the final price of the home. While the price reduction will not be too drastic, any reduction is good since you will have to make the repairs yourself down the road.

  If the homeowners suggest a reduction in the final price, you should consider the offer and find out how much the repairs will cost you. If it seems like a fair deal, then take it. If not, you can always ask for a larger reduction. Most buyers and sellers eventually agree on a price that will suit both parties.

- **Ask homeowners to pay for all closing costs**
  Another way to save money without relying on the homeowners to pay for the repairs is if they agree to pay the closing costs on both sides. This will free up some of your money so that you can make the repairs yourself.

  You may have to have a separate contract drawn up that will explain what the homeowners are responsible for paying, and what you are responsible for paying. This will make buying the home much easier.

  Any agreements that you make with the homeowners should be made in writing. Verbal agreements do not stand up in court, and are not common practice among real estate lawyers and agents when they are closing a deal. Your agent should make this clear to you at the beginning of the home buying process.

  Do not be discouraged if there seems to be a lot of paperwork. This is necessary and the usual standard practice for those who want to protect themselves from wrong doing and lawsuits later on.

The Final Walkthrough

On the day of the closing, you should have a final walkthrough whether you are purchasing a new home or an older home. Final walkthroughs are a way for you to determine if there is anything else you will need to discuss, get in writing, or have changed before you sign the paperwork.

The final walkthrough will include you, the homeowners, real estate agents, and if necessary, your lawyer. Unfortunately, many buyers skip the final walkthrough in anticipation of moving into the home quickly. But you should have one more walkthrough just to be sure.

The benefits of a final walkthrough include:

- Making sure all repairs that were conceded by the homeowners have been made
- Be sure additional repairs are not necessary
- Walls are intact
- Plumbing is intact
- Flush toilets in the home
- Garage door opener
- Test doors and windows
- All appliances that were remaining are still in the home
- Appliances are in good working condition
- Electrical systems are working by turning on all lights
- All junk is removed from the yard as per prior agreements

You will feel much better after the final walkthrough for many reasons. You will get to see first-hand the repairs that have been made, you will begin to see yourself living in the home, and you will be able to plan for the future in terms of what you want to keep in the home and what you want to remove.

In some cases, you will never meet the homeowners. If they have moved before putting the house on the market, you may be dealing directly with the homeowner's lawyer. It is still a good idea to ask questions about the home before signing the final paperwork.

The Closing

The closing is your last chance to ask for changes to the contract, to bring any concerns, and to ask the homeowners any questions you may have about the home and the property.

At the closing, you should bring:

- A notepad
- Financial notes and mortgage approval paperwork
- Signed paperwork you have received over the course of the deal
- Identification, and
- The home inspection report

At this meeting, you will be signing the paperwork that will make the home yours. This is a very exciting time, but you should maintain your composure to make sure that you are getting what you are signing for. If repairs have not been made, then you have the option to wait until they are complete.

When to Walk Away

Any time after the home inspection if you begin to have doubts about purchasing the home, you should contact your real estate agent and voice your concerns. Many first time home buyers need reassurance that they are making the right decisions. Your real estate agent will want the sale to go through, but they know that there are other properties they can show you , so they are not really losing money if you decide not to buy the home.

There are many reasons to walk away from a home sale. These include:

- A bad report from the home inspector
- The homeowners are unwilling to pay for necessary repairs
- You find another home that suits your needs
- The price for the home is too high
- You decide you don't like the neighborhood
- Loss of your job, or
- A medical emergency

Walking away from a home is not giving up on your dream of

ownership. Unfortunately, there are times in life when buying a home is not possible. If the financial strain is going to be too much, for example, then you should seriously consider finding a lower priced home or a smaller home.

If you decide to walk away from a home, you should give yourself a few weeks to recuperate before going out there and finding another home. You should contact:

- The real estate agent
- The lender, or
- The builder

Let them know of your decision and that you will be in touch when the time is right. Many times, after a bad report from a home inspector, it is just not worth spending the money on a home that will require a lot of repairs down the road. While all older homes will have some repairs, you should know the limits of what is acceptable and what will cost you too much money.

If you can get enough financing and you want to pursue the home regardless of the repairs that will have to be made, then go for it. Sometimes buying an older home and fixing it up can be a fun activity for everyone involved. Only you can make these crucial decisions. A home inspection will help you realize how much work and money may be involved if you decide to purchase the home.

6
Buying Your First Home

Financing your first home can be the most frustrating part of the home buying process. This is the time when you will figure out how to pay for the home. Most people have to take out a mortgage loan in order to afford the price. Which mortgage loans are right for you? How much of a down payment will be necessary? What is escrow?

You will have many questions about financing your first home. By knowing the facts, paying attention to interest rates, and looking into all of your mortgage options, you will be able to choose repayment terms that will fit your current income and allow you to safely make those monthly payments.

Types of Home Loans

Deciding which home loan is the right one for you will depend on what you qualify for and what your lender is willing to give you. There are a few types of mortgage loans, including:

- Fixed rate mortgage loans
- Adjustable rate mortgage loans
- Balloon mortgages, and
- Jumbo loans

You should be familiar with these loans so that you will be able to make an informed decision when it comes to financing your new home.

Fixed Rate Mortgage Loans

For first time home buyers who are on a strict budget, choosing a fixed rate mortgage may be the loan for you. Your monthly payment will never change for the life of the loan because you will lock into the interest rate given at the time the loan was processed. You can take out loans that range from ten to thirty years.

There are many advantages to taking out mortgage loans that have fixed rates. You will be able to create a monthly budget for yourself, you will never be surprised by the amount you will have to pay each month, and you will be able to lock into a low interest rate.

The disadvantages may not mean much to you now, but as your family or your income grows, you may want to refinance and pay less each month so that you will be able to afford renovations, vacations, and other luxuries. Since your mortgage is fixed, if interest rates drop, you will be trapped paying a higher rate. While you can refinance your mortgage, you will have to wait a certain amount of time, and even then there may be complications.

For those who have limited income, who have lower credit scores, or those who want the security of paying the same amount each month, then a fixed rate mortgage is the loan for you.

Adjustable Rate Mortgage Loans

If you expect to make more money in the next few years, and want to buy a bigger home, you may be interested in an adjustable rate mortgage. The major difference between an adjustable rate mortgage and a fixed rate mortgage is that the interest rate will vary year to year in an adjustable rate mortgage.

While the interest will be capped, you will still be paying more for each year that you own your home unless interest rates drop over an extended period of time. Most adjustable rate mortgages cannot be raised more than 2 interest points per year, and up to 7 points for the life of the loan.

These loans are good for those who want a larger home and who expect to increase their earnings each year to afford the increase. If you are in a position to take out an adjustable rate mortgage, you will be able to lock into a fixed rate that may be lower than your original rate. This is the main advantage of these loans. Most lenders will only give you two years to lock into a rate or the loan will remain adjustable for the life of the loan.

Balloon Mortgages

If you are only planning on living in your first home for a few years (usually five to seven), you should look into a balloon mortgage. These mortgages require that you pay them off in five to seven years. They have a lower interest rate that is fixed.

If, after the term of the mortgage has passed and you want to remain in the home, you will have to refinance and choose a fixed rate or adjustable rate mortgage to pay off the existing mortgage, as balloon mortgages cannot be renewed.

Only consider this mortgage if you are planning on moving after a certain amount of time or if you think you can pay the mortgage off in that amount of time.

Jumbo Loans

Most first time home buyers will not need to take out a jumbo loan unless they are buying a very large home. These loans are valued over $417,000 and are used to purchase land and a home. More collateral will be needed in order to qualify for one of these loans. The interest rates are comparable to fixed and adjustable rate mortgages and have the same payment terms.

Now that you know about the types of mortgages that are available, you should be thinking about which lender to use. With so many lenders out there, it may be difficult to sort through all of them and find the right one. Doing a little homework will help you get the lowest interest rate possible.

Where to Find a Lender

These days there are many places to find a mortgage lender, such as:

- Family or friends
- Your current lender

As you can see, finding a lender should not be too difficult. You may have to contact several lenders before you find a lender that will give you a loan that meets your needs. When you apply for a home mortgage loan, the lender will check the following:

- Your credit score
- Your credit history
- Your current income
- Income of a co-signer, if necessary
- References (professional and personal)
- Current interest rates based on the amount you are asking for
- Status of other loans you may have
- Number of years you have been eligible to work, and
- Number of years you have had credit

There are many factors that will go into your approval or denial of a home loan. You will have to be patient. You should contact a few lenders to see which ones will give you the best deal. Once the offers have been received, you will have to make some important decisions.

You should feel free to contact your lender at any time during the home buying process with questions and concerns you may have. Other important information the lender will need before granting you a loan include:

- The home inspection report
- The termite inspection report, and
- The home appraisal report

These reports are very important to a lender because they will tell the lender how much the home is actually worth and the types of damage that have lowered the overall value of the property. Lenders expect homeowners to remain in the home for at least five years. This will allow them to make a profit on the money they have loaned you. It is not worth it to them if you have to sell the home shortly after buying it because there is too much damage and you can no longer live there.

Applying for a Home Loan

When applying for a home loan, you will have to bring the following information to the lender's office, or if applying online, supply copies that are faxed to the lender. What you will need to provide:

- 2 years of tax returns (all pages)
- 2 years of W2 forms
- Your most recent pay check stub
- 2 months of bank statements (all pages)
- 2 recent 401K statements (if applicable) all pages

You will be asked additional questions that will help the lenders determine if you are able to pay the loan back on time. These questions include:

- Number of years renting a home or apartment
- Late payment on credit cards and other loans
- Active loans (such as student loans or car loans)
- Number of years at your current job
- Additional income
- Amount of the loan and number of years to pay it back
- Number of years living in an area
- Dependents that are living in your home
- Tax returns and bank statements

Applying for a loan can take a week or more. This is because background checks, credit checks, and references must be checked before the loan will be processed.

In the meantime, you should be concentrating on gathering your paperwork, calling friends and family that you want to use as references, and sorting through your papers in case you cannot find everything the lender requests.

If you do not have your back tax returns, you can contact the IRS and request them by year. Many times, lenders will need to see returns from at least three years ago. Bank statements and bill statements from the past year should be enough to secure a loan.

If you are turned down for a home loan, you will be notified as to the reasons why. This can be devastating, but you should find other lenders and try to apply again. If you have poor credit, you may need to go through a lender that specialized in granting loans to those with poor credit. You may have to pay a higher interest rate, but at least you will be granted a loan.

Reasons for possible denial include:

- Poor credit or not enough credit
- Length of time at your job is too short
- Income level for the amount of loan requested
- Loan default
- Failure to pay rent or other bills, or
- Too much credit

Applying for a home loan can be stressful, but if you have good credit, steady employment, and enough income, you should have little trouble qualifying for a loan.

What Not to do When Applying for a Home Loan

There are a few things you should not do after applying for a home loan:

- Buy a new car
- Begin a new job
- Buy new furniture or other large items using your credit cards
- Apply for a credit card, or
- Default on student loans or other loans

All of these actions will cause your credit score to change that will give lenders an inaccurate view of your spending habits and your overall credit score. If you take a job that pays you less than you noted on your home loan application, your lender may not agree to grant you the loan.

If possible, do not begin a new job until you have moved into your home. Try not to spend money on credit cards. Buy furniture and other items using cash, or wait until you have signed the final contract and are a homeowner.

How Much Can I Afford

While there are many items that will change this number, the most important answer is, do you have a budget? Most first time buyers have never put together a real budget. Use the following two forms to answer this question of what can you REALLY afford. The short answer lenders look for is what is called Debt to Income ratio or DTI. The second form will show you what your DTI will allow. In general, your total DTI should not exceed 43% of your gross income. While that statement might seem scary and technical, the following forms will make this a very simple math problem.

BUDGET

INCOME SOURCE	INCOME
Borrower Gross Income	
Co-Borrower Gross Income	
TOTAL GROSS INCOME	
TOTAL NET INCOME	
EXPENSE DESCRIPTION	**AMOUNT**
Rent	
Food	
Utilities (gas, water, electric, trash)	
Gasoline	
Cell Phone & Land Line	
Home Maintenance	
Dry Cleaning	
Housekeeper	
Child Care	
Visa, Master Card, Dept. Store payments	
Car Payments	
TOTAL EXPENSES	

TOTAL NET INCOME	
TOTAL EXPENSES	
EQUALS ABILITY TO SAVE	

Increase Your Chances for Approval

There are a few ways to increase your chances for loan approval that will also help you determine what you will be able to afford each month:

▪ *Pre-approval*

Many experts agree that applying for a loan **before you find a home and being pre-approved** will help you create a budget, buy a home that is in your price range, and help lenders make their decisions faster.

▪ *Ask for only the amount you will need*

One way to increase your chances for a home loan is to not ask for more than you will qualify for. This means you will have to look at your income level, the amount of debt you have, and the expected monthly mortgage expenses, because your lender will. Apply for the amount you will need and nothing more.

▪ *Pay off credit cards*

If you are thinking about buying a home in the next few years, you should prepare by paying off those credit cards and only using them for emergencies. Do not cancel your existing cards since this may actually lower your credit score. By showing you have a zero balance on your credit cards, you will be showing lenders that you know how to use credit wisely and you have been paying your cards off on time.

▪ *Always pay bills on time*

This includes your electric bill, rent, student loans, and other bills that you may have to pay each month. By creating a track record that can be traced, you will be showing lenders that you are a responsible person who deserves to have a home loan.

What Makes Up My Credit Score

Credit scores and the formulas that the three major credit bureaus use are a closely guarded secret. However, in general here are the five major areas that agencies look towards when determining your score.

▪ *Payment History-35%*

The most important component of your credit score looks at whether you can be trusted to repay money that is lent to you. This component considers the following factors:

o Have you paid your bills on time for each and every account on your credit report? Paying bills late has a negative effect on your score.

o If you've paid late, how late were you – 30 days, 60 days, or 90+ days? The later you are, the worse it is for your score.

o Have any of your accounts gone to collections? This is a red flag to potential lenders that you might not pay them back.

o Do you have any charge offs, debt settlements, bankruptcies, foreclosures, suits, wage attachments, liens or judgments against you? These are some of the worst things to have on your credit report from a lender's perspective.

- *Amounts Owed-30%*
The second-most important component of your credit score is how much you owe. It looks at the following factors:

o How much of your total available credit have you used? Less is better, but owning a little bit can be better than owing nothing at all because lenders want to see that if you borrow money, you are responsible and financially stable enough to pay it back.

o How much do you owe on specific types of accounts, such as a mortgage, auto loans, credit cards and installment amounts? Credit scoring software likes to see that you have a mix of different types of credit and that you manage them all responsibility.

o How much do you owe in total, and how much do you owe compared to the original amount on installment accounts? Again, less is better.

▪ *Length of Credit History-15%*

Your credit score also takes into account how long you have been using credit. How many years have you been using credit for? How old is your oldest account, and what is the average age of all your accounts? A long history is helpful (if it's not marred by late payments and other negative items), but a short history can be fine too as long as you've made your payments on time and don't owe too much.

▪ *New Credit-10%*

Your FICO score considers how many new accounts you have. It looks at how many new accounts you have applied for recently and when the last time you opened a new account was.

▪ *Types of Credit in Use-10%*

The final thing the FICO formula considers in determining your credit score is whether you have a mix of different types of credit, such as credit cards, store accounts, installment loans, and mortgages. It also looks at how many total accounts you have. Since this is a small component of your score, don't worry if you don't have accounts in each of these categories, and don't open new accounts just to increase your mix of credit types.

How Home Appraisals Can Affect Your Home Loan

Unfortunately, a home appraisal can affect the status of your loan. If the home appraisal comes under the selling price of the home, most lenders will not grant the loan. This can be heartbreaking, but there are a few solutions that may work depending on the rules of the lender. The following options are available:

▪ *The homeowner reduces the selling price*

Depending on the appraised value in comparison to the asking price, some homeowners will be willing to lower the price of the home if they need to sell quickly.

You should not count on this happening since many homeowners want to receive the price they are asking for. You may have no choice but to find another home.

▪ *A higher down payment*

Some lenders will grant you the loan if you agree to pay a larger down payment on the home and assume the financial risk. This is only an option if you can afford to pay a larger down payment. Do not risk your financial security in these cases; it is just not worth it.

▪ *Dispute the appraisal*

You can send a letter to your lender disputing the appraisal or have another appraiser determine the value of the home. You will have to pay for this second appraisal, which may or may not yield the same results. There is no guarantee that your lender will accept the second appraisal.

▪ *The mortgage timeline*

Most mortgages can be closed in 30 days. In today's market, it is not uncommon to run into delays with lenders that might take up to 60 days to close your loan. Some lenders close loans in as little as 20 days, while another lender across the street might take as much as 60 days for the same loan transaction.

▪ *Find another lender*

This is a last resort move because it will postpone the closing for another month or so, and there is no guarantee that the lender will accept the appraisal.

Since home appraisals are required by most lenders, you should find out during the loan application process the policies that the lender has when dealing with appraisals. If your lender will not accept a lower selling price, you putting down a larger down payment, or other solutions to a low appraisal, you should consider finding another lender just in case there are any problems down the road.

Home appraisals are based on the current value of homes in the neighborhood, homes that are comparable in size, the housing market, and the age of the home. While you can expect to hear different numbers from different appraisers, you will see that these numbers will usually not be too far off.

The only real benefit of a low home appraisal is that it will tell the homeowners to list the home for less money so that they will be able to sell it. In the meantime, you will have to find another home.

How Home Inspections Can Affect Your Home Loan

While a poor home inspection will usually not deter a lender from granting a home loan, you should be aware that some lenders will not grant a loan if there is termite damage or structural damage to the home due to water or age.

This will also lower the overall appraisal of the home, which could be another issue that lenders may have when deciding to approve a home loan.

If the home inspection is not favorable, ask your lender what will need to be done in order to rectify the problem. Many times removing the termites and correcting the water damage is all that will be needed. Many times homeowners will foot the bill for these types of repairs.

Additional Fees for Home Loans

You may notice that you have to pay small fees throughout your home buying experience. It seems that every piece of paper you sign, file, or request will cost you some money. Here is a list of fees that you may be charged:

- Credit report fee
- Loan discount fee
- Lender's inspection fee
- Appraisal fee
- Loan origination fee
- Mortgage insurance application fee
- Assumption fee
- Hazard insurance
- Title search, and
- Title insurance

These fees can add up, so you will want to be prepared and have a little extra in savings for when these fees come up. Some of these fees can be put off until the closing, but you should be planning for them in advance.

Good Faith Estimates

Many lenders have turned to good faith estimates that are supposed to help you afford your new home. Many of the above mentioned fees may be added up and paid at the closing.

When looking for a lender, you should compare good faith estimates to see which lender is the lowest, which are the highest, and which are in the middle. All too often, these estimates are too low. Some lenders will do this on purpose in order to get you to take out the loan. By comparing estimates, you will be able to get a better idea of which lenders are honest and which are not.

As a rule, you should expect to pay between three and five percent of your loan in closing costs. A good faith estimate will give you an idea of the final cost, but you should keep track of what everything costs and try to have extra money set aside just in case.

Escrow and Other Loans Terms
As you are going through the home loan process, you will run across a few terms that you will not understand. You should ask your lender to explain these terms so that you will fully understand the type of loan you are applying for, the lender policies, and other information that will be important throughout the life of the loan. Here are some common terms you may encounter:

- *Escrow*
While this term can mean different things in different situations, you will see it often when closing a home. If you place a down payment on a home, it will be in escrow until all the paperwork has been signed. The money is held by a neutral third party, such as another bank or escrow service, and will be distributed once the deal is over. You can ask your real estate agent about escrow services in your area.

- *Mortgage*
Even though you have heard of a mortgage before, you probably thought of it as the home loan you will be paying once you move into your new home. Technically, a mortgage is a lien on your home created by the lender. If you cannot make payments on your home, the lender will have the right to sell the property in order to gain the money that they have lost.

- *Foreclosure*

This is a term that refers to homes whose owners could not make payments each month. Once a lender has decided to sell the home, it will be in foreclosure. You should find out ways to work with your lender in case you miss a mortgage payment at any time. Having this knowledge in advance will make financial emergencies easier to deal with.

▪ *Mortgage Broker*
A mortgage broker is a person who does not work for a bank, but rather works on commission to match homebuyers with many lenders that may not be in your area. If you have poor credit, you may want to secure a home loan through a mortgage broker because you will have a better chance than going through a bank that only has one lender to choose from – themselves.

▪ *Points*
This refers to the interest rate on your loan. If you choose an adjustable rate loan, for example, your points may be capped each year so they cannot exceed a certain number.

▪ *Down Payment*
A down payment is helpful in several ways. It will lower the amount of money you will need for a home loan, it will allow lenders to see that you are responsible for paying off a mortgage, and it will move the home buying process faster. Most first time homeowners will put down no more than 20% for a down payment.

You do not want to overextend yourself by putting a huge down payment on a home because you may not have enough money to pay your mortgage, afford new furniture, or make home repairs.

▪ *Debt to Income Ratio*
This is one way that lenders will determine if you can afford your monthly mortgage payments on your current income. The lender will subtract all your reoccurring debt to determine how much is left for a mortgage payment.

This is why not buying a car or spending money on your credit cards is so important when buying a home. The less debt you have will mean more available money for your mortgage payment.

▪ *Private Mortgage Insurance*

If you cannot afford to put down more than 5% on a home, you may not be approved for a loan. But if you purchase private mortgage insurance, your lender may agree to give you the loan. This extra insurance will protect the lender in case you default on the loan by paying them at least 15% of the total loan value. This will cost you a little extra each month, but it may be worth it.

▪ *Credit Report*

Before you apply for a home loan, you should obtain copies of your credit report so that you can check for errors; see how much money you owe on credit cards and loans, and see what your credit score is. This is another way that lenders will determine if you will receive a loan.

There are three credit reports that you should obtain, because you will not know which one the lender will base their decision on. While the numbers from these credit reports should not vary too much, if you see any major discrepancies, you should contact the agency and have the mistake corrected. You are entitled to one free credit report per year by contacting the IRS for more information.

7

Making a Realistic Offer

By this point, you should have found a real estate agent, contacted a few lenders, and seen a few homes. If you have not made up your mind on a home yet, you should take your time and keep looking. But keep in mind that if you wait too long, you may end up in a bidding war with another buyer.

Making an offer on a home is a huge step. You will be taking on the responsibility of a mortgage, repairs, lawn care, and other chores that homeowners sometimes gripe too much about. While you should be cautious, you should also make a bid on a home that you really like within a week after seeing it. This will put your mind at ease so that you can think of all the other items you will have to get done before the closing.

What to do Before Making an Offer
Before you make an offer on a home, you should do the following:

- *Attend open houses*
  Attend as many open houses as you can in homes that are in the area where you want to live. This will give you the opportunity to see what is out there, the going price of homes in the area, and also give you a basis of comparison when looking at other homes.

- *Find out more about a property*
  If you find a home that you might want to buy, you should find out everything you can about the property first before making an offer. Visit the county clerk's office or land records office to see how much the current homeowners paid for the land and the value of their property. This will give you an idea of how much you should offer for the home. If the home is in an area that has seen better days, then you can make an offer that is less because when you sell the property someday, you may have to lower your price as well.

- *Find out more about taxes in the area*

  As a homeowner, you will be paying yearly property taxes, local taxes, school taxes, community dues, and other taxes that could drive your household spending through the roof. Before you commit to living in a certain area, make sure you understand everything you will be paying each year.

  Your real estate agent should have the neighborhood information that will help you decide where you want to move. You can also visit your local tax office and see how much the current homeowners paid in taxes last year.

  When you visit a lender, you will have to figure in your taxes as household expenses. This will be deducted from your income, which will leave you with less each month to pay your mortgage. Just because you have found a home that is within your budget, you may not be able to afford the taxes that come with it.

These suggestions will help you make the most informed decision possible when it comes to buying your first home.

How to Write a Purchase Offer

This is the most important step when making an offer to buy your first home. The purchase offer should outline everything you expect from the homeowner and what they can expect from you. You should include the following in your offer:

- Price being offered
- Amount of deposit on the home
- Amount of money you will be putting down on the home
- Contingencies (such as appliances that will stay, repairs that will need to be made, removal of items in the yard, etc.)
- When closing will take place
- Specify who will pay which fees, and
- Any reports that will be needed

Each of these categories should be explained in its own paragraph. You should try to be as specific as possible when writing up a purchasing offer. Each state has its own laws concerning contingency, amount of time a buyer has to respond to the offer, and fees that are to be paid. Be aware of these laws before sending your offer or you may end up with a counter offer or a rejection.

Have a lawyer or our real estate agent look over the purchase offer before sending it. They may have some advice or additional categories you should add depending on the age of the home, the neighborhood, and the laws that exist. If you make an offer that is reasonable, well written, and hard to break, then you will be on your way to buying a home.

Making an Offer

After completing your research, you will be ready to make an offer on your first home. You will have to visit your real estate agent to sign a formal agreement that will outline your offer and for how long you will be making this offer. Most agreements will give sellers three days to a week to consider the offer.

In this time, the offer may be accepted, rejected, or a counter offer will be made. You will have to decide what you will want to do next if the offer is rejected or another offer is made. If the offer is accepted, then you will have to contact your lender, home inspector, and make arrangements for your move.

Low or High Offers

Hopefully, by researching the neighborhood, the property, and the value of the home, you will be able to come as close to the seller's price as possible. Sometimes, though, this is not possible. There may be circumstances that may prohibit you from making an offer that is close to the selling price.

Low Offers

Low offers are usually the result of the selling price being too high, ignorance of the buyer, or the buyer not having enough money to pay the asking price. Whatever the reasons, you should be careful when giving a low offer to a homeowner.

If you have specific reasons for offering a lower price, they should be mentioned in the offer so that the homeowner has a better understanding of how you came to the price offered. In some cases, the seller may offer a counteroffer, which you can either accept or reject. But, if the homeowner feels insulted by the lower offer, they may just reject the offer and move on to another.

High Offers

The only time you should make an offer that is higher than the asking price is if other offers have been made. While this could be the beginning of a bidding war, if you offer just a little more than the highest bid, you may win. You should only do this if the property is worth it and you will be living in it for a long time.

If you make an offer that is high, then you will not leave any room for negotiation. Depending on the homeowner's circumstances, they may have been willing to go a little lower in order to sell the home. But since you made an offer that was higher than the asking price, you will end up paying more than you should have.

Many times, first time home buyers make the mistake of wanting a home so badly that they are willing to pay a few thousand more than the home is worth. This is money that could be used for a down payment.

Making the Right Offer

The closer you can come to the asking price, the better off you will be. Once the home inspection is complete, the homeowners may have to come down in price anyway because of the repairs that will have to be made.

Making the right decisions when buying a home are not always made quickly. You should play by the rules and just see what happens. If you get into a bidding war and cannot bid any higher, then it is best to let the home go and find another. You should not be a slave to your first home by buying one that is over your budget. There are many homes that are available if you keep looking.

How to Handle a Counter Offer and Offer Rejection

Sometimes, if you give homeowners an offer that is lower than their asking price, they may offer you a counter offer. This is usually an offer that is more than your offer, but a little less than the asking price.

- #### Counter Offer
  Depending on where you live, the laws pertaining to counter offers will vary. Typically, the number of counter offers is limitless, but no counter offer can be the same. While counter offers are usually concerning money, these offers may also contain the following:
  - o Ownership of appliances
  - o Repairs
  - o Time frames for closing, and
  - o Time frames for counter offers

Buyers and sellers may only have hours to accept, reject, or offer another counter offer after receiving one. This can be a very stressful process, especially if you are dealing with a seller that has other offers on the table. While most homeowners will reject an offer if it is too low or they have received another, some will try to get the most they can from the sale that can include the smallest items in the home.

If you are determined to buy a home, but still want a lower price after the buyer has reacted with a counter offer, you can try to find a price that will suite everyone's needs. If you are making a counter offer that does not make that much difference, you should weigh the odds that another offer has been made, the homeowner will reject your offer, and that time is ticking for everyone.

Try your best to accept the counter offer before making one of your own. Is it really worth losing your dream home over one or two thousand dollars?

Dealing with Rejection
The hardest part about an offer rejection is that the homeowner does not have to answer your offer. If you do not hear from the homeowner within a week, it is safe to assume they are not interested in your bid. While this can be frustrating, you will have to move on. Begin your house hunting again and try to stay positive.

If the homeowner gives you a response in the form of a rejection, they may site the reason why in the paperwork. If your offer was too low, they had another offer, decided not to sell, or want to wait for a higher offer, at least you can move on without wondering why our bid was rejected.

Considering Items in the Home
When you are writing your purchase offer, you should consider the items that you would like to keep and items you would like to have removed from the home. These items can include:

- Certain appliances (such as washer and dryer)
- Lighting fixtures
- Storage fixtures
- Single air conditioning units that fit into windows
- Hardware from windows and doors, or
- Pools

You should put these items in writing so that you will get them with the home. Some homeowners may try taking certain items with them either because they didn't know that you wanted them or because they were not supposed to be sold with the home to begin with. Be sure to obtain a list of items the homeowner is selling with the home so that you can compare it to your list.

This can also work in reverse. If there are items that you would like removed from the home or property before you move in, you should specify these in the offer. These items can include:

- Old patio furniture
- Mechanical equipment
- Old appliances, and
- Light fixtures

By putting all of these items in writing, you will be helping to move the buying process along. While the homeowners may not agree with everything that you may want to keep, it will be up to them if they want to continue the process. Having everything in writing will leave people with no surprises during the closing.

Understanding the Seller

One of the key elements of making a solid offer is having an understanding of the seller. Your real estate agent will be able to tell you a little bit about the seller that may help when trying to come up with a fair offer.

When deciding on an offer for the home, you should find out the following about the seller:

- How eager are they to sell their home?
- How long have they lived in the home?
- How many offers have they received?
- How many have they turned down?
- Have they lowered their asking price?
- Are they relocating to another area?
- Do they need to sell their home quickly?
- Are they waiting for their asking price?

What to do in a Buyer's Market

In a buyer's market, you will have more choices when it comes to the types of homes you can purchase.

Depending on how long the market favors the buyer, you will also have the luxury of taking your time because bidding wars are much less. When buying your first home, you should check out all your options. That home you couldn't afford a few years ago may be in your price range today.

When looking for a home in a buyer's market, you should do the following:

- Stay current with listings in your area
- Sign up for free email listings and newsletters
- Check out homes that have recently been reduced
- When making an offer, ask for closing fees to be paid for by the seller
- See if there are other offers, such as appliances that come with the home
- Ask for certain allowances (carpeting, roofing, siding, etc.)
- Do not be afraid to offer a lower price, and
- Ask for a shorter response time

In a buyer's market, homeowners may offer these options to you as incentive to buy their homes. They may also offer warranties on appliances that you should take advantage of.

There are dangers that you should consider when buying in a buyer's market, however.

- If you are not planning on living in the home for more than three years, you may want to wait until the market changes or plan to live in the home longer. Many times, market trends can last for a few years. If you need to move after a year or so, you may have difficulty finding a buyer and you may have to sell the home for less than what you paid for it.
- While most homeowners stay in their homes for at least two years in order to save money in taxes, marketing trends have been known to last longer. You should be prepared for this when buying your first home.
- Make sure a thorough home inspection has been completed before buying the home. If you decide you cannot live there after you have bought the property, you may have difficulty

selling it, and you will have to spend more money making repairs.

Even though you cannot predict how the market will change, you should consider a home that you can afford, that you will want to live in for a long time, and one that can be improved upon while you own it.

What to do in a Seller's Market

In a seller's market, you will have to play the game slightly different than you would in a buyer's market. In this type of market, there are many buyers who will want to buy homes that are attractive and priced within their budget. Homeowners will have their pick of offers to choose from so your offer will have to stand out in more than just price.

When looking for a home in a seller's market, you should:

- Make an offer that is close to the asking price or slightly over
- Send a pre-qualification letter from your lender with the offer
- Choose a closing date that is sooner rather than later
- Do not ask for too many contingencies
- Send a personal letter
- Promise more of a down payment, and
- Use a real estate agent that gets things done quickly

In a seller's market, you may also want to think about the dangers of buying a home. If you make an offer that is too high and you find out later on that the mortgage payments will be a struggle, you may have to sell. Depending on changes in the market, this may be more difficult than when you were looking for a home.

Buying your first home during this time may also be difficult because you will not be able to put much down, you may only qualify for a certain amount of money which may not be enough to compete during a bidding war, and you may be outbid by those who have more experience than you do.

When you decide to buy a home, you should be looking at your financial situation, the market, and the asking price for the homes you are interested in making an offer on. If you can wait a few months to see where the market is headed, then maybe this is the best way to save more money and find a home that is affordable. This is a waiting game that no one wants to play, but may be necessary, especially if this is your first home purchase.

Seller's markets and buyer's markets have their advantages and disadvantages, but in the end, the offer that you make will determine whether your offer will be accepted.

8

Contracts, Home Warranties and the Closing

Drawing up contracts, having the final walkthrough, and going to the closing are the last steps you will have to take when buying your first home. This is the time when having a real estate agent you can trust, and a little knowledge of home buying come in handy.

But, what about all of those other miscellaneous fees that will come up before and during the closing? You should be aware of additional fees when you apply for a loan and when you are closing on your new home.

Contracts

Your purchase offer was the first contract you will be involved in when you want to buy a home. You should refer to this contract during the closing period to make sure that your rights are covered and that you are getting everything you pay for.

By writing a solid purchase offer that outlines what you want from the homeowners, you will be protected in case of disagreements and other issues before closing. But a purchase offer is just one of many pieces of paper you will have to see and sign before you can move into your home. Other contracts include:

- Contingencies
- Builder contracts
- Mortgage contracts, and
- Closing agreements

These contracts may vary in length depending on the forms being used and the information that will have to be included.

Contingencies

Real estate contingencies can be added onto an existing contract or can be created as a separate contract depending on what you would like to include in the purchase offer. Contingencies can include a wide range of items, including:

- Home inspections and pest inspections
- Home appraisals
- Financing
- Septic system tests
- Appliances that will stay in the home, and
- Property surveys

Contingencies can make or break a sale, so you should be sure to use the correct forms when filing contingencies and to word them carefully.

You will need to include a resolution for repairs that may need to be done before you can move into the home. If it is agreed upon in writing that he homeowners will take care of all or some repairs that may be found during a home inspection, this will save time later on.

You should also include ways to get out of the deal that include loan denial, repairs that cannot be fixed, and lead, mold, or radon that is found in the home. Having a way out of the contract will save you money and time.

If you are buying a home that is for sale by owner, you should find an attorney or real estate agent that is willing to help you create a contingency list and edit it where necessary. Do not rely on the seller's agent because they are after their client's best interests and not yours.

Builder Contracts

If you are buying a new home from a builder, you will have to sign a builder's contract that states you have the financial means to pay for a new home, that you have decided on a location for your new home, and that you are ready to build.

You should hire an attorney at this point to go over the contract to see if there are any problems that will have to be ironed out before you begin building the home.

Mortgage Contracts

In order to complete your home buying, you will have to be approved for a mortgage by a lender and you will have to sign a contract in which you agree to an interest rate, monthly payment schedule, rate plan, down payment, and other fees.

These contracts are standard loan contracts that will explain the consequences of not paying your mortgage. You should read this paperwork carefully before signing anything.

Closing Agreements

These are the final contracts you will have to sign before you get the keys to your new home. You should read this paperwork carefully and be prepared to pay any closing costs at this time.

Home Warranties

If you are buying an older home, you may want to purchase a home warranty that will cover repairs that will have to be made during your first year of ownership.

While a home inspection will catch any immediate repairs, no one can foresee an oven falling apart or a dryer burning out. Since you may not have a lot of extra money left over after paying for closing costs, down payment, and mortgage payments, having extra insurance will allow you to make the repairs you will need.

Most policies will cost between three hundred and five hundred dollars. Coverage will begin the day of your closing and will last for a year. You will have the option of renewing the policy if you would like at that time. If you need to have an appliance repaired, you may have to pay a small co-pay at the time of the repair.

Not all policies are the same, so you should do your research to find the best deal. Compare the types of repairs that are covered under the policies and choose the one that fits your home.

Closing

When you finally arrive at the closing, you should expect to:

- Sign contracts,
- Do a final walkthrough
- Pay closing costs, and
- Get your keys

The closing can take an hour or two, but usually moves quickly because there is little left to do. At the closing you will probably meet the homeowners. This could be the first time you will meet them. This is a good time to ask if there is anything about the home you will need to know.

Sign Contracts
When you sign the contracts, read them carefully to make sure everything that has been discussed is in the contract. Ask questions that you may have at this time.

Final Walkthrough
The final walkthrough of the home will take place before or during the closing. This is the final chance for you to see the home before it becomes yours. Make sure the items on your contingency are in place so that you can sign the contracts.

Paying Closing Costs
Typically, the buyer will have to pay the closing costs associated with buying a home. But in a buyer's market, you may be able to add a contingency that states the seller will be responsible for all costs. This may appeal to sellers who want to sell their home quickly.

When deciding who should pay the closing costs, you should research laws that may be in place that dictate who pays for what. Many times, buyers and sellers will agree to split all costs including closing, home inspection, pest inspection, and home appraisal costs. You will have to negotiate with the sellers to see which you will be responsible for.

Get Your Keys
After signing the contracts, you will receive the keys to your new home. This is an exciting feeling and one that will be with you for a long time.

Conclusion
When it comes to purchasing a home you will find that it takes a long time. You will have at least seven homes shown to you before you make the decision to buy. There are some realtors who will show you that many in a day. How many homes that you see are completely up to you and how good your realtor is.

The realtor will ask you some basic questions about price and features, but a good realtor will find you a house within three shows. Why? Because everyone knows that a good realtor will be able to match a home with the couple's personality. When you go with your realtor to purchase a home you should get plenty of rest the day before and you need to eat a hearty meal because you don't want to quit early in the day because you don't feel well.

At last, you will want to make sure that everything goes according to plan so that you can have a smooth adjustment into owning a home.

BONUS CONTENT

Important Information about Charleston

CITY FACTS:

Population:	130,113 / 787,643 area
County:	Charleston
Time Zone:	Eastern
Area Code:	843
Zip Codes:	29401, 29403, 29406, 29407, 29409, 29412, 29416, 29424, 29425, 29492
Mayor:	John Tecklenburg
Total Area:	127.53 sq. mi.
Founded:	1670

GOVERNMENT OFFICES:

City Offices	www.charleston-sc.gov	(843) 965-4055
Parks & Rec Events	www.ccprc.com	(843) 795-4386
Police Department	www.charleston-sc.gov	(843) 577-7435
Public Library	www.ccpl.org	(843) 766-2546
Chamber of Commerce	www.charlestonchamber.org	(843) 577-2510
Public Works	www.charlestoncounty.org	(843) 202-7600
City Hall	www.charleston-sc.gov	(843) 577-6970

SCHOOLS:

Stono Park Elementary		(843) 763-1507
Oakland Elementary		(843) 763-1510
Ashley River Creative Arts Elementary		(843) 763-1555
Harbor View Elementary		(843) 762-2749
Charles Towne Montessori		(843) 571-1140
St. Andrew's School of Math and Science		(843) 763-1503
James Island Christian		(843) 795-1762
Porter-Gaud		(843) 556-3620
Ashley Hall		(843) 556-3620

DAYCARE CENTERS:

Smart Cookies Early Childhood Center		(843) 852-2242
Le Petite Academy		(843) 556-5873
Loving & Learning Educational		(843) 795-9183
Wonderful Beginnings		(843) 225-5501
Audacy Creative Arts Preschool		(843) 637-3135
Saint James Day Care		(843) 762-8287

SPORTS & ACTIVITY CENTERS:

Charleston Parks & Rec	www.ccprc.com	(843) 795-4386
Charleston City Recreational Services	www.charleston-sc.gov	(843) 724-7327
St. Andrew's Parks & Playground	www.standrewsparks.info	(843) 763-4360
Bees Landing Recreational Center	www.charleston-sc.gov	(843) 402-4571
James Island Recreation Complex	www.charleston-sc.gov	(843) 795-5678
Arthur B. Schirmer Jr. Tennis Center	www.charleston-sc.gov	(843) 402-4571

NEWS:

The Post and Courier	www.postandcourier.com	(843) 577-7111
Charleston City Paper	www.charlestoncitypaper.com	(843) 577-5304

UTILITIES:

Charleston Water System	www.charlestonwater.com	(843) 727-6800
Dominion Energy of SC	www.sceg.com	(888) 333-4465
WOW! (Internet, TV & Phone)	www.wowway.com	(843) 225-1000
Comcast (Internet, Cable & Phone)	www.comcast.com	(855) 319-2121
AT&T (Internet, TV & Phone)	www.att.com	(855) 293-7676

ENTERTAINMENT:

Charleston Municipal Golf Course	www.charleston-sc.gov	(843) 795-6517
Shadowmoss Plantation Golf Club	www.shadowmossgolf.com	(843) 556-8251
Charleston Gaillard Center	www.gaillardcenter.org	(843) 724-5212

CHURCHES:

Seacoast Church	www.seacoast.org	(843) 375-1089
St. Phillip's Church	www.stphillipschurchsc.org	(843) 722-7734
St. John's Lutheran Church	www.stjohnscharleston.org	(843) 723-2426
First Scots Presbyterian Church	www.first-scots.org	(843) 722-8882
First Baptist Church	www.fbcharleston.org	(843) 722-3896
Sacred Heart Catholic Church	www.sacredheartcharleston.org	(843) 722-7018
Grace Church Cathedral	www.gracechurchcharleston.org	(843) 723-4575
Mother Emanuel AME Church	www.motheremanuel.com	(843) 722-2561
French Huguenot Church	www.huguenot-church.org	(843) 722-4385
Unitarian Church of Charleston	www.charlestonuu.org	(843) 723-4617

PUBLIC PARKS:

James Island County Park	www.ccprc.com	
Brittlebank Park	www.charlestonparksconservancy.org	

TESTIMONIALS

Phenomenal service!

zuser from Summerville, SC

I recently worked with Ellen and her team at Movement Mortgage for purchasing my first home. If you have never purchased before the mortgage process can be quite daunting. Ellen and Movement made the process very quick and easy for me and were beyond helpful in finding the perfect loan for my needs. I would highly recommend using Movement, they were courteous, helpful, friendly, and efficient throughout the process.

Closed Jul 2017

Ellen Frazier

JH from Charleston, SC

She was extremely helpful, knowledgeable in all aspects of the lending process. her staff was also super helpful and friendly. I would definitely refer her to all my friends needing mortgages for their first, second or third homes.

Closed May 2017

Positive experience, highly recommended

vicandallan from Mount Pleasant, SC

My home buying experience exceeded my expectation! Everyone was very helpful throughout the entire process. I appreciate their expertise and would highly recommend Ellen Frazier to anyone looking to finance a home.

Closed Jan 2015

Highly Recommend

edupee from Mauldin, SC

Organized and great with time management! Felt like we were her only priority at that time. She did what she could to help with saving money and what was in our best interest with a VA loan.

Closed Jan 2016

Very nice, helpful, and knowledgeable

taylor from Charleston, SC

Ellen addressed all my concerns throughout the mortgage process. She walked me through every step of the process. She was very accessible and knowledgeable. I would recommend her to anyone for a seamless process.

Closed Aug 2015

Ellen Frazier was the best

cherylann from Allen, TX

I couldn't have asked for a better mortgage broker. She was very detail oriented. Very knowledgeable. She was very helpful with providing all the necessary paperwork.

Closed Apr 2017

Couldn't have been more professional

sports4639 from North Charleston, SC

Super professional, affable, and courteous...made sure every step of the process was smooth sailing. Would highly recommend to anyone in the Charleston area.

Excellent knowledge and personality

user from Charleston, SC

Ellen walked up through the entire process start to finish explaining everything and left no stone unturned happy to start this next chapter in life thanks to her!

Closed Jan 2017

Professional, Knowledgeable and Straight Forward - Helpful

zuser from Allen, TX

I was considering a refinance loan and Ellen Frazier walked me through the paces and at the end of the conversation, I was able to develop in my own mind the advantages and some disadvantages that I had not considered. Her assistance helped me greatly in my making decision and that attention to detail saved me lots of money.

Extremely Professional

victoriageib from Charleston, SC

Extremely professional and courtesous to work with. Really took the time and made sure I understood all of the nuances of the process. I very highly recommend to anyone in the area! Thanks again!

Great to Work With!

patrick from Charleston, SC

They are very knowledgeable and and easy to work with. Super attentive to detail and great communication throughout the whole process. Highly recommend Movement Mortgage!!!

Previous Client Facebook Post:

I"m going to need a lot of cards because I'm giving them to every body! It will become my hobby forever and ever because there is no other FINER company! If you need lender, STOP you have found the right one, the easy part is done, and house buying will become a charming adventure..stress free and easy..in fact, if you were even just thinking if you need to buy a house, go ahead, do it NOW, this lender has your back!

She is a very caring individual who want the best outcome for her and the Movement Mortgage has to offer.

B. Holden 10-2019

How process could have been more enjoyable: Ellen and her Loan Officer Assistant, Jordan, provided a very positive and enjoyable experience through their knowledge and expertise. They were extremely efficient during the entire process and I was comfortable, never concerned, with their timely communication through email, phone calls, and occasional texts. A phenomenal mortgage re-fi experience!

26501705R00052

Praise for *The Real Two Hearted*

"This is a celebration of place, a warm family memoir and an acute biography of the river whose name Hemingway made famous. The author's keen observations and thorough research make this a unique book about a special corner of Michigan."

—**Dave Dempsey**, environmental advocate and author of
The Waters of Michigan and *Great Lakes for Sale*

"Bob Otwell has written a fascinating and insightful tribute to Michigan's most famous river. As a hydrologist and engineer, he presents an authoritative and carefully researched study of the Two Hearted and its watershed. But he has the heart of a poet, too, and his love for the river shines through on every page."

—**Jerry Dennis**, author of *The Living Great Lakes*

"Anyone whose first big purchase is a 17-foot canoe is my kindred spirit. I'm willing to follow Bob Otwell wherever he goes, especially to Michigan's Two Hearted River. This is a loving history of the UP, full of forestry, hydrology, lumber history and conservation. Whether you're a Hemingway fan or an armchair naturalist, you'll feel part of the family at Boggy's Camp on the Two Hearted River."

—**Heather Shumaker**, author of *Saving Arcadia*

"This is more than a memoir.... Otwell delves into the ecology and history of this lightly populated corner of Michigan's far north, from glacial retreat that formed the Great Lakes to 19th century logging that scarred the landscape and modern efforts to restore it.... He introduces the reader to indigenous tribes, lumberjacks, fly fishermen and colorful 'yoopers' who share his love of this idyllic spot—while expressing fear and hope for its future."

—**John Flesher,** retired northern Michigan
correspondent and environmental reporter,
The Associated Press

the
REAL
TWO HEARTED

For my dad, Bill Otwell.
He loved my mom, our family, books, history, fishing,
and Up North.

the
REAL
TWO HEARTED

Life, Love, and Lore Along
Michigan's Most Iconic River

BOB OTWELL

MISSION POINT PRESS

Mission Point Press
2554 Chandler Road
Traverse City, Michigan 49696
www.MissionPointPress.com

Printed in the United States of America

Cover Art: *Two Hearted Twilight* by Kaye Krapohl, 2010, from the collection of Kennard and Judith Weaver
Map: *Two Hearted River Watershed* by Colleen Zanotti

Softcover ISBN: 978-1-961302-80-8
Hardcover ISBN: 978-1-961302-79-2

Library of Congress Control Number: 2024912781

Contents

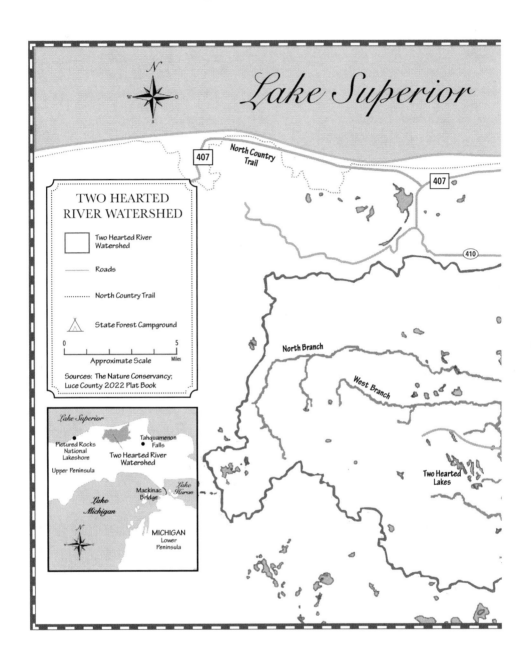

TWO HEARTED

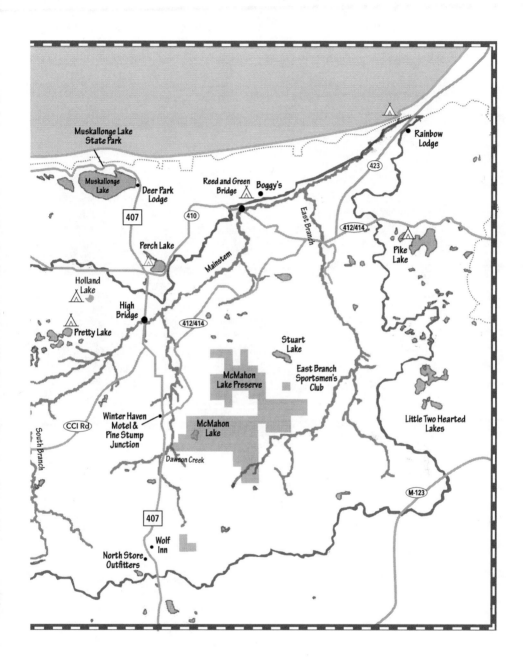

RIVER WATERSHED

THE RIVER

CHAPTER 1

FINDING BOGGY'S CAMP

There is something exceptional about the Upper Peninsula of Michigan. It is hard to put into words; it is one of those "*you know it when you see it*" feelings. Travelling over the Mackinac Bridge always gives me a feeling of stepping back in time, where the pace of life slows a bit and folks wave as they pass on the road, whether they know you or not. My wife, Laura, and I appreciated that, and the wildlands, small quaint towns, and the remoteness that the bridge inspires.

We had always hoped to spend more time in the U.P. and own a place to grow attached to. The wild rivers and forest trails kept drawing us back as we camped, hiked, skied, and canoed. Laura and I were often frustrated because the campgrounds we preferred to stay in were full. With a growing family, we were less flexible, and we started exploring. We visited properties for sale, some located next to rivers and creeks, vacant land where we envisioned building our getaway. But many of these properties were a disappointment. The lands had been part of recent timber sales, the large trees harvested, with only scrub littering the ground where the forest had been.

One weekend in April 1991, grandparents gave us the opportunity to go on another reconnaissance visit. Our oldest daughter Claire was five years old, and Annie was three. Nothing was panning out. One last opportunity arose when we read an ad for a "Cabin on the Two Hearted River" in *Michigan Out-of-Doors* magazine. We stopped at a gas station near Tahquamenon Falls to use a pay phone to inquire about the cabin and see if it was still available. Luckily for us, in those days people answered the phone. Cathy Robinson, the realtor, said she thought the owner was at the cabin and that we could just stop by for a visit.

It was Sunday afternoon, the kids at home, grandparents needing relief from the little ones, jobs waiting for us on Monday morning. Our real life was catching up with us and we started for home. But we kept talking about the cabin, and not too far down the road we decided, what the hell, let's look, and we turned around. It was one of those seemingly minor life decisions that has major consequences.

We drove back north to Luce County Road 500, then over 15 miles of rough gravel roads, through some scenic forests, but also through some cutover jack pine. As we crossed the Two Hearted River and approached the cabin, the trees got larger, the forest more majestic. That first sight of the cabin, overlooking the river and flanked by a white picket fence, was undeniable; it produced a gut feeling of "*oh my goodness, this is the place.*"

We knocked on the door and were invited in by the owner, Jim McCarley. We were first greeted with a small, dark entryway with firewood stacked in the corner. Inside, the cabin was a refuge from the cold spring day, warmed by the wood stove. The cabin was a throwback. The living room had rich, dark pine paneling that was easy on the eyes. The paneling consisted of wide tongue and groove boards and extended across the ceiling all the way from the floor. The stuffed chairs were old but looked comfy. Electric lights hung from the ceiling, along with propane lamps on the walls, situated in places convenient to reading. Three large windows illuminated the room. A large black wood stove was centered in the room. Several animal heads hung on the walls, the most impressive being two large bucks, with interlocking antlers and a story all their own.

A small dining area overlooked the river at the end of the room. It seemed to be a converted porch with cheap imitation sheets of wood paneling. A long, sturdy pine table with a bench along the wall filled the space, where ten people would easily fit for a meal. Three large windows provided views of the river below. Around the corner and through a small doorway was a kitchen. The kitchen had mismatched white wood cupboards,

Boggy's Camp on the Two Hearted River, October 2023.

a big country sink with Formica counters, and a low ceiling with white tiles. There was a propane refrigerator and a four-burner stove, with oven. Laura noticed duct tape smoothing the connection between the sink and the counter. Two windows let light in, and a door led outside.

In the entryway at the front door were bunk beds, with four more sets of bunks through a low doorway to a bunk room. The bunk room was also paneled with the same dark pine and had a lofty ceiling. The bunk room had two nice windows and a door to the outside. Jim indicated the bunk room was moved there from a closed CCC camp that was built in the 1930s. Laura worked for the Youth Conservation Corps in the western U.P. the summer after high school. She had lived in an old CCC camp that summer and recognized the construction. Off the bunk room was a small bathroom with a sink and a toilet. The sink drained to a bucket underneath.

Exiting the rear door of the bunk room were two connected outbuildings, a pine-paneled sauna, and an old shed. We have since learned it would not be a U.P. camp without a sauna. The shed was full of tools, supplies, and a big old propane generator.

Inside, the cabin had a distinctive—not unpleasant—musty odor. Probably a combination of dead animals (hanging on the walls and in them), old furniture, and being closed up most of the time. This odor remains. It is apparent when we first arrive and then disappears. We call it the Boggy's smell. When we return home from a visit, our dogs will retain the pleasant smell in their fur for a few days.

We talked more to Jim about the camp, which had recently been listed to be sold as is. We then walked down to look at the river. The steelhead were running, and the bank had several fishermen, standing as sentries above the river. One of them, John, said to me, *"Don't buy this place, the river gets way too high in the spring, and the camp will eventually wash away."*

We ignored John and shortly thereafter had a cursory inspection done, made an offer, and finalized the purchase. What we bought was a small rustic cabin with a significant sag in the roof. The cabin had cedar shake siding, was covered with rolled roofing, and it came with the name Boggy's Camp painted on a sign by the front door. The 1984 MDNR County Map Book also labeled Boggy's Camp one of the historic recreational camps in northern Luce County.

Camps in the U.P. are what we call cabins elsewhere. Historically many start out as encampments without permanent structures, just canvas tents. The camp had a rich history, we would later learn.

Boggy's Camp was located on two acres, sitting above a steep sand bank of the Two Hearted River, surrounded by the Lake Superior State Forest. Our youngest daughter was born four months after we took over the camp. She was referred to as Baby Boggy until she was born, at which point she was named Julia Leigh. She lost the nickname immediately!

Laura and I had often dreamed about owning property on a canoeable river. When we were first married and living in East Lansing, we looked at a house for sale on the Grand River. The house was south of Lansing near Eaton Rapids. It was inconveniently located and did not fit our needs, but it was on a river. We passed.

The first possession Laura and I bought jointly when we were still dating in college was a 17-foot-long Mad River Explorer fiberglass canoe. It was the most expensive item she had ever purchased. This meant a serious commitment. Our first canoe outings were in winter on the Red Cedar River in Lansing, a little unsettling for novice canoers. We paddled Lansing area rivers, then when we moved north to Traverse City, we paddled Northern Michigan and U.P. rivers, and did some canoe camping in Ontario.

Canoeing together can be a test for a relationship. Ours was a little tippy at first, but over time we grew comfortable in our positions, Laura in the bow and me in the stern. In August 1984, to celebrate our first year of marriage, we took the canoe and our six-month-old black lab, Chester, and paddled and portaged into a secluded little lake in Ontario for a weeklong getaway. Not seeing another soul the entire time, we were attracted to this silent sport. On another memorable trip, we took our two young daughters, 80-pound Chester, and all our camping gear in the canoe for a trip across Lake Mijinemungshing in Lake Superior Provincial Park. With not a lot of freeboard to spare, we carefully made our way across the large lake.

Annie, Laura, and Claire, headed out to canoe camp on Lake Mijinemungshing, Lake Superior Provincial Park, 1991

After purchasing Boggy's, we canoed often on the Two Hearted. The Two Hearted River is wild and isolated. The river is what first attracted us to Boggy's Camp, that little white cabin overlooking the eternal flow of the river. Near our camp, the river varies from deep pools to shallow, gravel riffles. A lush smorgasbord of flowers, grasses, alder, dogwood, mature white pine, big oaks, and maples fills the riverbanks. The river meanders around many bends, calling you further downstream to explore around the next corner.

Since we bought the place, we have wondered about this little piece of land: what year was the cabin built? Who was Boggy? Who has visited the camp? Before the camp was built, what was the land like? What animals have walked across this land, and do they still visit when we are away? In what ways have the forest and river changed? What is the history of this place? What is its future?

The Michigan Department of Natural Resources, in December 1973, published the Two Hearted River Natural River Plan. The plan described the Two Hearted as follows:

> *The Two Hearted flows uninterrupted by dams for 35 miles through a "wilderness like" watershed in northern Luce County. In addition, five major tributaries add 80 miles of streams in the system. These streams contain a variety of interesting wildlife, ecological systems, and scenic attractions. The mainstream and South Branch are particularly well known for their fishing quality. Roughly 44 percent of the stream system mileage is in state ownership within the Lake Superior State Forest. It is recommended the mainstream of the Two Hearted and its five major tributaries, North, South, East and West Branches, and Dawson Creek from their headwaters to the mouth of the river at Lake Superior be included in Michigan's Natural River System as a "Wilderness River."*

There are currently 16 rivers in the Michigan Natural Rivers program, two in the Upper Peninsula (U.P.), and the rest in the Lower Peninsula. The Two Hearted River has the state's only "Wilderness River" designation. As described later, more of the watershed is protected now than it was in 1973. We learned that this lightly touched watershed has only one paved, plowed road, and few permanent human residents. In the late 1980s, the National Park Service considered the Two Hearted for designation, one of three finalists for a proposed "Wild River National Park."

We realized this would not only be a special place for the Otwell family, but a special place in the shrinking world of wild places. What are the current threats? Why has this watershed been so untouched? Do the current land-use controls go far enough? What about climate change?

In the 30-plus years we have owned the camp, we have come to learn much about the river and the surrounding land. We have enjoyed the camp in all types of weather, and have numerous stories, many shared in our Boggy's Camp Journal. I set out to write this book to learn more: more about the river; more about the undeveloped Two Hearted River watershed; and more about the people and events that have shaped this place we love. And because of all of that, I have learned more about myself.

CHAPTER 2

WHERE IS THE
TWO HEARTED RIVER?

Hemingway's Confusion

So, where do I begin to describe the Two Hearted River? People love its aura. This may have begun with Ernest Hemingway's beloved story, set in the Upper Peninsula, *"Big Two-Hearted River."*

Hemingway's story is loosely based on his own background. Growing up in the Chicago suburb of Oak Park, at the south end of Lake Michigan, he spent much time in Northern Michigan. His family had a cottage on Walloon Lake, near Lake Michigan's northern end.

The story is about Nick Adams returning to one of his favorite fishing spots, seeking peace from the wilderness after experiencing the horrors of the First World War. Hemingway himself visited the U.P. in 1919, after returning from the First World War. He published the short story in 1924.

Nick takes the train to Seney and is actually going to fish on the Fox River, which flows through the small village of Seney, not the Two Hearted. Seney is about 12 miles southwest of the South Branch of the Two Hearted. This sleight of names was not realized for some time. Sheridan Baker may have been the first to identify the actual river as the Fox. He published that opinion in the *Michigan Alumnus Quarterly* in 1959.

Early on, the confusion over the river created an influx of anglers to the real Two Hearted River. Gerald Elliot, a writer for the *Grand Rapids Press*, met a prominent Newberry businessperson Joseph Rahilly. Rahilly was the owner of the local Ford dealership and a member of the Michigan Conservation Commission. Elliot interviewed Rahilly, published in an undated news clipping, "Hemingway's Wrong River."

> *"Did Ernest Hemingway ever fish the Two Hearted?" The question provoked a tirade that would have scorched this paper. "What brought that on?" I asked. Rahilly and his friends around Newberry had a fishing-hunting lodge well up the Two Hearted and had built a private road to it. When Hemingway's story appeared in a magazine, Rahilly thundered every s.o.b. in the country who owned a fly rod was up on their river in two weeks and ruined the fishing there for all time.*

Hemingway simply liked the "poetry" of the name better than the Fox River. Even though he may not have been fishing the Two Hearted, Hemingway's prose can put us in the setting of any wild river:

> *He sat on the logs, smoking, drying in the sun, the sun warm on his back, the river shallow ahead entering the woods, curving into the woods, shallows light glittering, big water-smooth rocks, cedars along the bank and white birches, the logs warm in the sun, smooth to sit on, without bark, gray to the touch; slowly the feeling of disappointment left him.*

Hemingway spent many summers of his youth on Walloon Lake near Petoskey. Hemingway fished on nearby Horton Creek, and on other nearby trout streams. He made the foray to the Fox River with a few friends in August of 1919 just after turning 20. They travelled by train. That same summer he also went with friends to the Pigeon River Country, another Northern Michigan area with wild and remote trout streams (the Black River, the Pigeon River, and the Sturgeon River). The Pigeon River Country is only about 40 miles from Walloon Lake. He in fact spent a few days on the Sturgeon River just before his 1921 wedding to Hadley Richardson.

What I appreciated from reading the *Big Two-Hearted River* was his love for fishing, but also his love for wild country, and for simply being outdoors. Much of the first half of the story is more about camping in the remote U.P. than fishing. For folks who love to travel, carrying a small tent to pitch, the details of camping can fill up the day. These activities are many: find a camp site, unpack, find a spot to pitch the tent, pitch the tent and prepare sleeping quarters, collect wood and build a fire, prepare and eat food, sleep, build fire in the morning for coffee, eat, take down camp, pack up, and then do it again. Here again is Nick on his fishing trip in the *Big Two-Hearted*.

The ground rose, wooded and sandy, to overlook the meadow, the stretch of river and the swamp. Nick dropped his pack and rod-case and looked for a level piece of ground. He was very hungry, and he wanted to make his camp before he cooked. Between two jack pines, the ground was quite level. He took the ax out of the pack and chopped out two projecting roots. That leveled a piece of ground large enough to sleep on. He smoothed out the sandy soil with his hand and pulled all the sweet fern bushes by their roots. His hands smelled good from the sweet fern. He smoothed the uprooted earth. He did not want anything making lumps under the blankets . . .

Out through the front of the tent he watched the glow of the fire, when the night wind blew on it. It was a quiet night. The swamp was perfectly quiet. Nick stretched under the blanket comfortably. A mosquito hummed close to his ear. Nick sat up and lit a match. The mosquito was on the canvas over his head. Nick moved the match quickly up to it. The mosquito made a satisfactory hiss in the flame. The match went out. Nick lay down again under the blanket. He turned on his side and shut his eyes. He was sleepy. He felt sleep coming. . . .

The river was clear and smoothly fast in the early morning. Down about two hundred yards were three logs all the way across the stream. They made the water smooth and deep above them. As Nick watched, a mink crossed the river on the logs and went into the swamp. Nick was excited. He was excited by the early morning and the river. He was really too hurried to eat breakfast, but he knew he must. He built a little fire and put on the coffee pot.

Nick was there because of the river, but he was also inspired by the natural surroundings and simple pleasures. Sleeping in a tent and sitting around a remote campsite, one experiences primeval feelings that hark back to an era when people lived much more in tune with the natural environment. Laura and I, 100 years after fictional Nick, still enjoy the pleasures of tent camping. Our nylon tent is lighter, more water- and bug-proof. If I tried to torch a mosquito with a match, it would burn right through our tent screen.

There is another, more recent use of the "Two Hearted River" because of the name. Bell's Two Hearted Ale is America's best-selling IPA. The brew, started in a small brewery in Kalamazoo, Michigan, in the 1980s, is now available in party stores all over the country. The river name is used to identify a Michigan product with ties to the U.P. and trout fishing.

The original label on the beer had a sketch of John Voelker, who wrote under the pen name Robert Traver. He was a Michigan Supreme Court Judge, fly fisherman, and U.P. author. He authored many books, including *Trout Madness: Being a Dissertation on the Symptoms and Pathology of This Incurable Disease by One of Its Victims; Trout Magic;* and *Anatomy of a Fisherman.* His most famous book, *Anatomy of a Murder*, was a best seller and became a Hollywood movie. The movie garnered seven Academy Award nominations in 1960.

Ladislov Hanka, a Kalamazoo artist and friend of Larry Bell, drew the Two Hearted Ale label along with other beer labels. On his website, Ladislov describes his love for fishing, his connections to Hemingway, and connections to Voelker.

Like Hemingway and Nick Adams, John Voelker too was a part of the vision I'd received among the mosquitos and skunk cabbages of Horton Creek. His writing had fed my soul at a formative time and several years later I began to feel a need to honor that. Though it seemed presumptuous of me to intrude on the aging master's privacy, I still wanted to meet him face to face—to make the trip to Frenchman's Pond and do some sketches. I began to make inquiries among fishing buddies who'd met him and they directed me to Pauly's Rainbow Room, a modest tavern in Ishpeming. There, the master storyteller and former jurist could, with luck, be overheard making provocatively dismissive pronouncements about bait fishermen and perhaps be induced to have a drink or go fishing. I knew then that I had to make the pilgrimage without further delay.

Ladislov tracked down Voelker and sketched him in his favorite bar in Ish-peming, Michigan. They used the sketch on the Two Hearted Ale label, and everything was fine until Voelker died. His widow did not appreciate her husband's portrait on a beer can. The label was changed to that of a brook trout, also sketched by Ladislov. That label is still on the beer today. The beer is one of my favorites. Not because of Hemingway or Voelker, but because I like the taste of the beer, and of course, the name.

A "Hemingway Society Headquarters" plaque has hung above a door-way at Boggy's since we bought the place. I always thought it was some cheap tourist item with goofy plastic fish. Turns out there actually is a Hemingway Society and Foundation, established by Hemingway's widow, Mary, *"for the purposes of awakening, sustaining an interest in, promoting, fostering, stimulating, supporting, improving, and developing literature and all forms of literary composition and expression."* The society meets biannu-ally and has had local meetings in Traverse City, Michigan (1983), and in Petoskey, Michigan (2012). On recent examination of the plaque, it is handmade. The plaque is inscribed with quotes written on it by hand from the *Big Two-Hearted River* story. The fish are not trout. As I have learned more about Hemingway's exploits on Northern Michigan remote rivers, the plaque seems at home in Boggy's cabin, on the banks of the real Two Hearted River.

On Google, search results for "Two Hearted River" are dominated by Hemingway's story and Bell's Two Hearted Ale. Google searches are fo-cused on buying something. I did not want to buy a book or a beer, just learn about the history and natural resources of the real Two Hearted River.

The Big Lake—the Lake Superior Watershed

The Two Hearted River is in northern Luce County, in the eastern portion of the Upper Peninsula of Michigan. The Two Hearted River flows into the south shore of Lake Superior, west of Whitefish Point. Boggy's Camp is about one mile south of Lake Superior. We enjoy hiking across state land to visit the big lake and walk along its beaches. A special treat, because of the proximity of our camp, is the roar of the surf, audible at our camp, when the north wind blows.

The stretch of Lake Superior that we walk to is very remote. It is miles

Julia, Laura, and Marta are standing near the edge of the shore of Lake Superior in March 2018. The mounds of ice visible are about 100 yards offshore. These ice mounds are located on top of submerged sand bars and stack up with accumulated ice each winter to heights of 20 to 30 feet.

Blaise, Jesse, Sarai, Claire and Laura on the shore of Lake Superior on a windy day in August 2023. This photo is taken at about the same location as the above winter photo. A different day, a different world.

in either direction from where people have public beach access. The mouth of the Two Hearted is six miles to the east, and Muskallonge State Park is six miles to the west. We very seldom see others on the beach.

Lake Superior is the largest freshwater lake in the world by surface area. It contains 10% of the world's fresh surface water and has an area of 32,000 square miles. Its deepest point is at 1,330 feet, and winds can generate waves over 30 feet high.

The lake receives water from 200 other rivers around its shoreline. The largest are the Nipigon in Ontario and the St. Louis in Minnesota. Two of the larger rivers entering the lake from the south in Michigan include the Sturgeon and Tahquamenon Rivers. Another source of significant inflow, because of its large surface area, is water that enters the lake as precipitation (snow and rain).

Small volumes of water also flow into the lake from two places outside of the Lake Superior watershed: Long Lac and Ogoki. The Long Lac and Ogoki diversions, located in northern Ontario, divert water from the Hudson Bay watershed into the Lake Superior basin. The Long Lac diversion began in 1939 and the Ogoki diversion began in 1943. Ontario Power Generation operates the diversions to improve capacity to generate electric power.

Water leaves the Lake Superior watershed through the outflow of the St. Marys River, and through evaporation. Evaporation is a significant part of the water balance in the Great Lakes because of their large surface area, especially when strong winds blow frigid air over warm waters in autumn. The Soo Locks on the St. Marys River in Sault Ste. Marie opened in 1855, allowing larger ships to reach Lake Superior. That, and the expanding copper and iron ore discoveries in the western U.P., accelerated ship traffic on the big lake. In 1876, the Two Hearted River watershed received its first permanent structure with the construction of the Two Hearted River Life Saving Station on the shore of Lake Superior. The site at the river mouth was chosen in 1874 and plans and specs were prepared.

Funding for the nation's lighthouses dates to 1789, when the United States Lighthouse Establishment was created and operated under the Department of the Treasury. The Whitefish Point Lighthouse was built in 1849, one of the first on Lake Superior. Whitefish Point is about 25 miles

Two Hearted River Life Saving Station, circa 1920
Source: Sterling McGinn Photograph Collection

east of the mouth of the Two Hearted. The steamer *City of Cleveland* was grounded in 1864, and in 1869 a schooner *W. W. Arnold* broke up, both at the mouth of the Two Hearted. These shipwrecks and others in the area prompted a response.

The shipwreck coast is a common term for the stretch of lakeshore between Whitefish Point and Grand Marais. The northwest winds generate huge waves on the Big Lake along this unprotected coastline. Four life saving stations were authorized in 1874 for eastern Lake Superior: Deer Park (Muskallonge Lake), Two Hearted River, Vermilion Point, and Crisp Point.

The Two Hearted station was located on the beach just west of the mouth of the Two Hearted River. This station was considered one of the important stations in the days of sailing vessels and it was responsible for rescuing 1,000 sailors. The life saving station was closed in 1921 and the buildings were torn down sometime after 1940. Some concrete remnants of the station are still visible. Below are two firsthand reports from the United States Life-Saving Service.

May 25, 1885—during a thick fog the steamship Algoma, *of Owen Sound, Canada, when off Two Heart River, Lake Superior, stranded on the bar, about three-quarters of a mile west of the Two Heart River Station, (Tenth District) Lake Superior. She was bound from Port Arthur to Owen Sound with a cargo of wheat, flour, and general merchandise. In addition to her crew of fifty-two persons she had 60 passengers. The keeper of the station, with his crew, put off in the surfboat, and boarded her at 11:00 in the morning, within twenty minutes after she struck. He advised the captain to send part of his cargo ashore to lighten the vessel, but later thought he could get off by shifting some of the cargo aft. All hands therefore set to work and helped shift cargo until 3:00 o'clock in the afternoon, when the keeper induced the captain to change his mind and order some of it taken ashore. The steamer's boats were then lowered, and, with the assistance of the surf boat, the unloading proceeded until half-past 5, when the vessel floated. At about 3 o'clock in the afternoon the keeper and crew of the Muskallonge Lake Station also arrived with their surfboat and aided in the work. The cargo was reloaded by half-past 8, and the steamer proceeded on her course, without any damage of consequence. The following letter of thanks was received by the General Superintendent:*

Steamship Algoma, Owen Sound, May 27, 1885.
Dear Sir: Coming down Lake Superior, from Port Arthur, bound to Owen Sound, on Georgian Bay, Monday the 25th instant, during a dense fog, and trying to work clear of heavy ice, we grounded abreast of Two Heart River, Lake Superior. Capt. Moses Chartier, of Two Heart River Station, came immediately to our assistance. When the fog cleared off, Capt. H. Clary, of Muskallonge Station, twelve miles distant, sighted us and came to our aid. With such help we were soon afloat, without suffering any damage. I must say that both the life-saving crews cannot be praised too much for the manner in which they performed their duties. Their assistance to us was invaluable, and it affords me a great deal of pleasure to be able to thus speak of them.
"I am, yours, very truly"
Jno. S. Moore, Captain

The Two Hearted River Watershed

The Two Hearted River is unique because it is one of the most undammed, untrammeled, undeveloped, unpopulated rivers on the United States's side of the Great Lakes watershed. There is a significant interplay between the Two Hearted River and Lake Superior, and the watershed is affected by its proximity to the big lake. Summers are cooler, especially close to the lake. In fall and winter the warmer lake moderates cold Canadian winds that blow from the north. The average winter temperatures range from 9 to 17 degrees Fahrenheit—the average summer temperatures range from 62 to 73 degrees Fahrenheit. The average annual total precipitation is 32 inches. Our camp is cooler in the summer, warmer in the winter, and receives more snow than Newberry, 30 miles inland.

To provide some technical background of the Two Hearted River, I reviewed several good reports with extensive information on the river and surrounding lands, starting with the 1973 Natural River Plan. In addition, there is *Two Hearted River: Leland Anderson*, Michigan Dept. of Natural Resources, October 1973; and *Two Hearted River Watershed Hydrologic Study*, Michigan Department of Environmental Quality, January 2007. Also, the extensive *Two Hearted River, Watershed Management Plan (WMP)*, produced by the Superior Watershed Partnership, May 2008, and updated in 2020.

Many of the improvements contemplated in the 2008 WMP have been completed. One primary focus of the WMP was to remove sediment from the river. Sediment, primarily sand, fills the voids in the gravel beds that trout and salmon rely on for laying their eggs. The projects reduced the annual sediment transport of over 600 tons per year. The projects also improved connectivity for 35 river miles. Stream connectivity can be cut off by improperly placed and maintained road culverts. These obstructions can affect the flow of water, the transport of nutrients and organic matter, and fish migration.

Five major tributaries make up the Two Hearted River system: the North Branch, West Branch, South Branch, Dawson Creek, and East Branch. The mainstream starts after the confluence with the South and West. Folks claim the name "*Two Hearted*" comes from these two primary tributaries, the beating heart of the main river.

The South, West, and East branches and Dawson Creek have swampy areas in their upper reaches, with beaver dams historically affecting water levels and vegetation. The two Spile Dams—one on the West Branch and the other on the East Branch—along with the Hemlock Dam on the South Branch, and the Hunter Dam on the mainstream near the South Branch, were all built as water control structures. Prior to 1915, these structures were used for log drives. Loggers built the structures out of wood. There is little remaining evidence of their existence.

The mainstream of the Two Hearted has a series of shallow sandstone ledges near the High Bridge on County Road 407. Farther downstream, the river flows through a valley that has isolated wetlands, dogwood and alder along the river, and spruce, balsam, cedar, and white and red pine on the banks, along with maple and oak. After the Reed and Green Bridge, the river meanders east with many oxbows. This is the stretch of river where Boggy's Camp is located. Many of the steep sand banks have exposed sand. There are many ancient white pine trees along the banks that escaped the saws of the 19th century loggers because of their inaccessibility. There are also many maples that glow yellow, orange, and red in the autumn.

The Ojibwe name for the Two Hearted River is "Niizhoodenh-ziibi," meaning "twin river." Many Indigenous names are being recaptured to honor Native Americans and the resources they relied on. The Boardman River was named after one of the forefathers of Traverse City, Harry Boardman. He came to town in the 1840s, bought land, and started cutting down trees. He despoiled the river that would eventually bear his name. He never took residence in Traverse City, but his name survives. I live in the Boardman Neighborhood, just east of Boardman Avenue. The Indigenous name for the river was the Ottaway, and that name is slowly working back into our local vocabulary.

The Two Hearted, as Hemingway observed, is a wonderful name, and honors the Ojibwe river name. Dawson Creek, one of the main tributaries, is a name that should change. Dawson was one of the logging camp owners who decimated the watershed and water quality with uncontrolled logging. An Ojibwe name should replace Dawson Creek.

The Two Hearted watershed is relatively flat, with its highest elevation sitting about 350 feet above Lake Superior. Wetlands are an important part of the uniqueness of the area. Freshwater wetlands provide water sources to streams, and provide shade, flood storage, wildlife habitat, and water quality protection. Wetlands cover over 40% of the watershed land area.

Wetland soil characteristics form when soil is under conditions of saturation, flooding, or ponding. Under natural conditions, these soils (also called hydric) are saturated or inundated long enough during the growing season to support the growth and reproduction of wetland vegetation. Under these saturated conditions, soil microorganisms can use all the oxygen in the soil, changing its color and appearance. If the saturation is common throughout the growing season, the plants decay more slowly, and a layer of peat is formed. Hydric soils occupy about 65% of the watershed and support the wetland communities found in the upper reaches of the Two Hearted watershed. Beavers have historically helped back up the tributaries and expand the time and extent of the saturation.

CHAPTER 3

RIVER FLOW

A Thick Layer of Snow

I have never seen snow like I have on our spring trips into Boggy's. We normally like to wait until March, after snowmobile season, to ski in. At that time there is plenty of daylight, and still lots of snow. Picnic tables at the campground have chest-high mushroom caps of snow. Three to four feet of snow shrink the cabin in height, and a good coal shovel is necessary to open doors. We have learned from experience to store the shovel in an accessible location, not in the shed. We have seen drifts of snow near our camp as late as Memorial Day.

Snowfall greatly affects the hydrology of the Two Hearted watershed. The largest flows in the river occur each spring, as the snow melts. The wetlands and the steady cold summer groundwater base flows are also affected by this increase in total annual precipitation which comes from the lake effect snow, in addition to normal storm system snow and rain.

Bob, Laura, Claire, Annie, Julia, and Chester to celebrate Bob's 43rd birthday. Early snows this winter, even in TC. Everything had been covered with snow since early November. Luce County Road commission plows County Road 410 until November 30 through deer hunting season. We decided we

could drive in (just flurries predicted for this weekend). We drove in, no other
car tracks, 2" of fluffy stuff. At Reed & Green bridge about 6", we drove in
all the way. Brought up 5 pairs of skis. We all skied on Saturday, even Julia.

It snowed and snowed and snowed on Saturday. Would we be able to drive
out? I was worried. On Saturday, Bob used the car to pack a sort of take-off
ramp and pointed the car down a slight downhill. A foot of fresh snow. The
burb came through, the last car on 410 for the year.

Boggy's Camp Journal, Laura, December 1–3, 1995

On December 9, one week later, Sault Ste. Marie recorded a record 5 feet of
snow in a 24-hour period. The National Guard was called in to assist with
snow removal. We could not have driven out through that. We did wonder
how much snow Boggy's got during that same storm, and worried about
the old cabin's roof.

This undeveloped area of Luce County gets a lot of lake-effect snow.
Lake-effect snow is common across the Great Lakes region during late fall
and early winter. This snow occurs when frigid air blows across the open
waters of the Great Lakes. As the chilly air passes the warm waters, moisture
is transferred into the atmosphere. The transfer is greatest when there is a
significant temperature differential between the warm water and frigid air.
The moisture-laden air rises, and clouds form and grow into narrow bands
that can deliver two to three inches of snow per hour.

Lake Superior is 300 miles across if one stands at the shore north of
Boggy's Camp and looks to the northwest towards Canada. The north and
northwest winds over the warmer lake pick up substantial moisture. We are
never sure how much snow we get each winter at Boggy's, because there are
no snow reports anywhere close. The amount of snow that builds up each
winter is considerable because of the high snowfall amounts in combination
with months of below-freezing temperatures.

We skied up. It was really hard and long six miles. Annie and I had to carry
up backpacks and it got really heavy. The day we got here, we had to shovel a
bunch of snow. We had to make a snow toilet, because the other one froze. The
next day we read a lot because Annie and I were in a reading contest at school.

We also made an igloo. All four of us worked on it, Annie, Daddy, Mommy
and I. What we did was we dug out chunks of hard snow, and put them on

*top of each other, and then pile wood on the top. When we finished Annie and
I had a cracker party in our igloo. We also shoveled off the roof and Annie and I
slid down. I had lots of fun on this vacation.*

Boggy's Camp Journal, Claire, age 10, March 15, 1997

Claire and Annie, March 1997.

Water on the Move—Hydrology

I have always been interested in creeks and rivers, starting with tramping
along Tonquish Creek with friends as a kid growing up in Plymouth, Michigan. We would grab sticks to pole vault across the creek, spot an occasional
snake, and catch frogs and butterflies. Snake grass was plentiful, and we enjoyed its special properties of connected pieces, like little tubes. In the summer, sometimes the creek would stop flowing, and we could catch crayfish
hiding under rocks. This creek wound through our neighborhood, a block
from my home.

My introduction to the natural world—and how it interacts with flowing water—came from this creek. I visited other natural areas with my
family to fish, camp, and hike. But this was a place I could visit daily by
myself and get to know. I remember one day I saw a small red dragonfly I
had never seen before. I thought it was something rare and incredibly special. It was, at least in my small world.

Fast forward 10 years, and I am studying hydrology as part of my Civil Engineering curriculum at Michigan State University. After graduation from MSU, and a master's degree from the University of Michigan, my first real job was to work on flood forecasting for a consulting firm in Southern California. They had a contract with the Federal Flood Insurance program to delineate and map the predicted 100-year flood boundaries for several communities. Having never lived out west, I was so surprised to see that the rivers I would be analyzing were dry—bone dry—most of the year. This helped in making the physical measurements needed regarding the size of the river channel and bridge piers to run hydraulic computer models. But I thought, "*What is the concern with flooding here?*"

Unlike western rivers, the Two Hearted is always flowing and has ever since the river valley was cut during the glacial retreat. The Two Hearted is a perennial river, where precipitation is always surplus. The water is stored in small lakes and wetlands, and in the soil, draining out slowly as groundwater. The water flows into small creeks and eventually into the main branch. The hydrologic cycle describes the fate of precipitation as it falls to the earth. It may:

- Be intercepted by trees and other vegetation, never reaching the ground;
- Infiltrate into the soils, to be taken up by vegetation, and then transpirate back to the atmosphere;
- Be evaporated from the ground surface, small depressions, or water bodies;
- Infiltrate into the ground, enter the groundwater system, and eventually flow into a surface water body. If the surface water body is a stream or river, this is described as base flow;
- Run off over the ground surface, filling in depressions, and then eventually entering directly into the surface water body;
- If the precipitation comes in the form of snow, follow the above paths after it melts. In addition, sublimation is a process where snow changes state directly from a solid to a gas and rises into the atmosphere.

Only one of these routes is visible to humans: the surface runoff. In steep, rocky terrain, runoff is the major contribution to the river and flash floods can happen because there is nowhere else for the water to go. In addition, significant runoff can occur in urban watersheds, where much of the land is impervious, covered by roads, parking lots, and building roofs. In flatter, sandy, undeveloped watersheds like the Two Hearted, runoff is a minor component in the summer, and even heavy rainstorms will be mostly absorbed by the land like a sponge.

My first hydrology textbook showed graphs of runoff (a plot of river flow over time at a point) from two watersheds, one a mountain stream in Hawaii, and the other the Manistee River in Michigan. The first was erratic, with rainfall instantly converted to stream flow. The second graph was flat, with precipitation absorbed into the gently sloped, sandy watershed.

Sublimation can be significant in watersheds like the Two Hearted where there are many conifers. The snow held up in the branches will be exposed to sun and wind, both of which increase the rate of sublimation. The snow transforms from a solid to a gas, and the moist air blows away.

I recently observed this phenomenon in our backyard in Traverse City. We had lost most of our winter snow accumulation, then we received an eight-inch late spring snowfall. The snow could not penetrate through a large spruce in our backyard and was held up in the branches. The next day, the snow disappeared from the branches, and a bare spot appeared. The eight-inch snowfall was already gone from the shadow of the tree. Sublimated.

A hydrologic study is an evaluation of the relationship between stream flow and the various components of the hydrologic cycle. The study can be as simple as determining the watershed size in acres and estimating the average stream flow. A more detailed study may involve developing a computer model to quantify the relationship between rainfall, peak flows, flood timing, land use, soil type, watershed slope, and watershed size. The Michigan Department of Environmental Quality completed a hydrologic study of the Two Hearted watershed in 2007. The study was conducted to help understand the watershed's hydrologic characteristics, to help inform the watershed management plan, and to look at historic impacts.

The Two Hearted River is surrounded by a watershed that is all forest and wetland. There is no agricultural or urban land use. The authors of the hydrologic study stated, *"do not expect this watershed to undergo long-term hydrologic changes that affect surface runoff volumes or peak flows."* These changes can include increased impervious surface or a change in vegetation.

Some of the larger rainfall events caused by climate change will influence the watershed. When I studied hydrology in the 1970s, the 100 years of rainfall and runoff data were deemed sufficient to predict the likelihood of large floods. For example, what is the magnitude of the 100-year flood? This is a flood, that, based on statistics, will happen once in 100 years. Over the past 50 years, hydrologists have become better at predicting the effects of the components of the hydrologic cycle, but the recurrence interval of rainfall events has become less certain. The warmer atmosphere holds more water, and rainfall events have become larger. Now, instead of using all the rainfall record, hydrologists are using shorter periods, with more recent data.

Big Spring Flows

Owning a cabin perched above a river makes the rise of the river a regular concern. We have seen the river at flood stage in the spring, and it can be scary high. We had been keeping an eye on a huge white pine leaning over the river at the "plumber's bend," a sinuous stretch of the river with rapids. We regularly walk to this area and canoe to it, about one-half mile upstream of Boggy's. The tree died, and then was ripped from the bank during the spring flood of 1996. This tree was recognizable, and we found it the next summer downstream of Boggy's, high on the bank, entwined with other trees.

Leaning white pine at the plumber's bend finally falls in 1995. Branches extend across the river, but a small opening remains for canoes at the base.

We often see evidence in the spring of the tremendous force of the river at high flood stage. Some photos on the web or TV regarding the aftermath of a tsunami or hurricane will remind me of some of these trees hung up on the bank after a spring flood. We quickly drop any thought of canoeing the turbulent river during those spring flow conditions.

A United States Geological Service stream gage was previously located near the mouth of the Two Hearted River. This gage provided continuous flow data from 1973 to 2013. Based on the gage data, average spring flows near the mouth at Lake Superior are 1,000–1,500 cubic feet per second (cfs). The peak flow on record is 3,350 cfs, on April 19, 2002. Average summertime low flows are about 100–200 cfs. Why the term *cfs*? This is a standard English unit utilized by scientists and engineers who study rivers. One cfs is 450 gpm (gallons per minute). An average garden hose flows at about 10 gpm. One can see the river is carrying lots of water, even at summer low flow, which is around 45,000 gpm.

The significant difference between spring and summer flows creates large differences in water level. In front of Boggy's, we regularly measured about a six-foot difference between river height in the summer and spring, based on a benchmark I had put on a large red pine on the bank. This red pine, and our benchmark, have since been swept down the river. The river does not want to be measured. In addition, we have seen evidence of high-water levels farther up on the bank, when we were not there. This evidence represents closer to a ten-foot difference in water level between summer and the largest spring flows. As a comparison, the Boardman/Ottaway River near Traverse City only fluctuates about two feet between summer low flows and storm-driven flows.

Based on peak flow data for the USGS gage and other data, the 2007 hydrologic study determined that the Two Hearted River watershed is a snowmelt-driven system. This is apparent if you spend time there. A snowmelt-driven system has a steadier flow than a storm-driven system. However, a rain-on-snow event, where rain and snowmelt simultaneously contribute to runoff, can produce dramatic flow increases in the spring. The runoff from the rain and snowmelt can occur with saturated and/or frozen soil conditions when the ground can absorb or store less water. This results in more overland flow to surface waters than normal. The heavy snow cover in the Two Hearted watershed does help to reduce significant frozen soils by insulating the ground all winter.

We experienced one unusual event in 2018. October rains drove the Two Hearted to reach flood levels normally only seen in the spring during snowmelt.

In Newberry, a two-inch rain was recorded in early October, and then two rains of over one inch each were recorded a few days later. We were up at Boggy's for the rain and the river rise:

> *Arrived Wednesday afternoon with a heavy rain following us in from Newberry. It rained and rained and rained the rest of the day and throughout the night. But Bob was able to grill BBQ chicken for dinner. Upon arrival, we were greeted by spectacular peak fall color display! And the river the highest I've ever seen it. Come daybreak it was still coming up. The lone red pine on the bank surrounded by flowing waters. The water reached steady state on Thursday/Friday and started to drop a little on Saturday. . . .*
>
> **Boggy's Camp Journal, Laura, October 10–14, 2018**

Information is now being collected by Lake Superior State University from instruments located in the Two Hearted River near the Reed and Green Bridge. These gages, installed in 2020, continuously measure river height, temperature, and conductivity.

River Hydraulics

Flowing water, whether in the small creeks I played in in my youth, or the large, fast flowing rivers Laura and I observed in British Columbia, have always fascinated me. We canoed the Fraser River a few years ago in Prince George, British Columbia. We were staying with friends of friends who owned two canoes. We got to the riverside and Laura and I were unsure if we wanted to get into the rolling, boiling waters of the Fraser. We went ahead and enjoyed a quick trip down to the edge of town. One new experience for us was that we could hear something, a constant drone rubbing on the canoe. We could not see anything, but it turns out it was glacial silt rubbing on the bottom of the canoe as the river swept past us.

Rivers flow due to gravity. Water from precipitation enters the river along various paths, then simply tries to get downstream. Dams do not stop rivers; they just slow them down. The dams store water, but they eventually let the water continue downstream. Beavers dam streams to create a safe, submerged environment for their homes. With their excellent hearing, they can hear slight trickles in their dams, and work to close them.

A small stick thrown into the river can tell us much about flow speeds and direction, even showing little back eddies where the water in a small section of the river will travel upstream. Fish use these back eddies to rest, or to travel upstream. Canoeists and kayakers use them also.

Energy of a River

The water, as it enters a river and becomes flowing surface water, has potential energy. The potential energy is immediately converted to kinetic energy, the energy that results from motion. Vegetation, sticks, stones, and the friction of the bottom all work to slow the river. The river continues its downward flow. Ever floated down a river in a canoe or inner tube? Thank kinetic energy. Kinetic energy can be seen clearly during flood conditions. Trees, debris, even cars can be observed flowing downstream in an urban river during severe storms, moved by the energy of the river.

A common way to use kinetic energy to the advantage of our society is to harness it. Dams are constructed to slow the flow of a river and create an elevated pond. The potential energy in the resulting pond is then converted to kinetic by providing an outlet where the energy can be focused. Ancient peoples used the flow from dams (mill ponds) to move large grindstones to mill grain. The loggers used waterpower to move logs and turn saws. More recently, water has been harnessed to turn turbines and generate electricity in many locations around the world.

River Flow Profiles

One matter I have pondered lately, based on the recent historic high-water levels of the Great Lakes, is how the elevated levels affect the river at Boggy's. In the summer of 2019, Lake Superior reached its all-time high-water level. Most of the rivers in the Lower Peninsula of Michigan, and many in the U.P., have mild slopes and therefore these rivers flow at what hydraulic engineers term "subcritical flow." This means that the flow velocity in the river is less than the wave velocity. The wave velocity is the velocity a wave resulting from a disturbance would move, relative to the moving water. If you throw a stone in a river, the ripples move out in circles. If ripples move upstream of where you tossed the stone, this would be a river with a mild slope. The ripples are moving faster than the river itself.

The basic rule of mild slopes is that the river water level surface is only affected by what is happening downstream. The river does not know what is happening upstream. As rivers flow into the Great Lakes, or another lake, the lake level is reflected up the river. This is termed downstream control. The river is affected by the downstream lake until it either 1) encounters a non-natural control structure (like a dam or weir) before the lake, or 2) it encounters a natural control like a rapid or waterfall, or 3) the river asymptotically approaches its steady state flow level some distance upstream.

Since there are no control structures downstream of Boggy's to the mouth, the Two Hearted reaches its natural river level some distance upstream of the mouth. That distance can be calculated, based on the slope of the riverbed, the river cross-section, and the river flow rate. The effect of changing Lake Superior levels would be noticed only relatively close to the mouth. The Lake Superior level does not affect the river at Boggy's, about 10 river miles upstream of the mouth. Some of the fast-flowing rivers of the western U.P. have supercritical flow, where the rivers are flowing faster than the wave velocity. These rivers would have upstream control over the water surface profile. They would not care what level Lake Superior is at when they tumble into it.

What Is a Hydraulic Jump?

While describing river surface profiles, an interesting phenomenon that most of us have seen, but may not understand, is a hydraulic jump. Hydraulic jumps can occur naturally but are also used by hydraulic engineers to dissipate energy coming out of a spillway built for a dam outlet. The flow is supercritical, moving quickly down the steep spillway, with a lot of energy. To dissipate the energy, a spillway is designed to slow the water and create turbulence to reduce the kinetic energy. This turbulence takes the form of a hydraulic jump, where the water goes from a steep flow profile, and "jumps" up to a mild flow profile. Controlling the jump allows the designer of the dam to force it to occur in an area of the stream protected with concrete, not in the natural river downstream which would then be eroded.

An example of a hydraulic jump can be seen in your kitchen sink. Take your dirty dishes out of the sink and turn the faucet on so that the stream hits the flat, horizontal sink bottom. The water flows in a smooth sheet, radiating out in all directions. In this region, the water is flowing at a supercritical velocity. After the water flows a few inches, it will "jump" up to subcritical flow because of the friction of the sink bottom. The turbulence in this little standing wave in the transition zone reduces the energy of the water.

Hydraulic jumps can also be seen at weirs which are constructed to help monitor river flow. A weir is a barrier built across a river or stream to raise and control the water surface. When a river is forced to flow through critical depth, with a concrete-armored river section, a consistent stage-discharge relationship can be determined. This allows a simple water level measuring device to determine river flow. Stage-discharge simply means that if you know the level of the water in the river (stage) you can determine the flow of the river (discharge). If there is a natural bottom to the river, erosion can alter the stage-discharge relationship.

I studied open channel flow in engineering school at Michigan State University. In front of the administration building, there is a broad crested weir that forces the Red Cedar River through critical depth, with a controlled hydraulic jump downstream. This is a popular place for students to sit and watch the river, the ducks, and other students. At high river flow rates, kayaks and surfboards can ride the large standing wave.

Kayakers playing in hydraulic jump (standing wave), Red Cedar River, Michigan State University. *Source: Power of Water, Lansing*

Hydraulic jumps can be observed in even mild rivers with intermittent rapids. As the river flows over and around boulders, the water backs up slightly and then speeds around the boulder. To slow down after the boulder, it must jump back to its former profile, and the turbulence caused by the hydraulic jump is visible and audible. So, what is a babbling brook? Just a beautiful little energy dissipater, following the laws of physics.

Stream Morphology

The shape and behavior of a river or stream is a function of a watershed's precipitation, topography, soils, flora, fauna, and geology. Engineering projects can have a significant impact, along with past and present land uses. The historic logging that occurred in the watershed in the late 1800s denuded the stream banks. Logs were floated to the mouth, gouging the sandy riverbanks as they travelled downstream.

A stream's ability to move sediment—both size and quantity—is related to the stream's slope and flow volume. The steeper the slope the faster the flow of the stream. Steeper reaches move larger material, such as stones and pebbles, and the flatter sections of the river tend to accumulate sediment. The melting of the large snowpack lets loose in the spring with a sudden warm-up. In the Two Hearted River watershed the runoff moves large volumes of not only sand, pebbles, and stones, but also trees, branches, and other woody debris. This debris can cut into the stream banks and start a new process of tree root ball removal and exposed sand banks. The Two Hearted River, from the Reed and Green Bridge to the mouth, has been cleared of tree blockage for many years to allow canoe passage. The surface of the Two Hearted River often freezes in the winter. Ice chunks can further carve stream banks as the ice breaks up in the spring.

Many riverbeds tend to flatten as they near the downstream end, causing the river to meander. As a river meanders, sand is deposited on the inner bank, and sand is removed from the outer bank. The sand is eroded on the outer bank due to lateral erosion, along with undercutting of the bank. There are also secondary currents that move sediments in the river from the outer bank towards the inner bank.

As this process continues, the meander increases, and the two concave banks get closer, forming what looks from above like an oxbow. The narrow neck of land between the banks can then be overtopped by a flood or

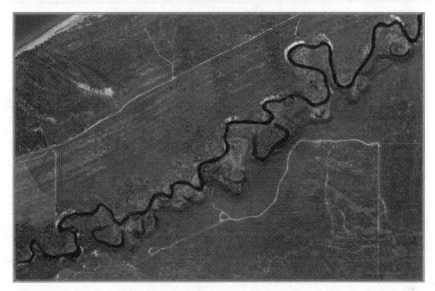

Two Hearted River near Lake Superior, showing oxbows in the river, and isolated oxbow lakes. *Source: Google Maps*

eroded away due to continued erosion. The river straightens, and the old opening to the oxbow gets cut off by deposition. The photo above shows the Two Hearted River going through a meandering oxbow in the upper right part of the photo. The photo also shows a few former oxbows, sometimes called oxbow lakes, that are cut off from the flow of the river except at flood stage.

Immediately upstream of Boggy's is an old oxbow lake. When the river is high enough in the spring, water flows around its historical path. Later in the spring, this low area gets separated from the river, and provides a stagnant source of water that the mosquitos love. By summer, the area dries up. I am not sure when this was part of the mainstream, but the isolation and steep banks helped preserve some majestic white pines from the logger's ax.

CHAPTER 4

POWER OF THE RIVER— EROSION AT BOGGY'S CAMP

Ihave been battling erosion of the sandy bank of the river in front of Boggy's for the past 25 years. The bank at our place is about 20 feet high and consists of sand and gravel. To help design a plan, I spoke with Steve Largent of the Grand Traverse Conservation District (GTCD) about the erosion along our bank. Steve and the GTCD have been doing soil erosion projects on the Boardman (Ottaway) River near Traverse City for many years. Steve described the utilization of tree revetments to stabilize the toe of the slope. He also suggested adding topsoil to the slope to grow grass. He said if you do not stabilize the toe, the slope above the toe will never become stable. The toe is that portion of the bank that is normally just above the river level. I really liked the idea of the tree revetments—bioengineering— and helping nature fix the damage that man and nature have caused.

I spent 30 years studying and practicing civil engineering. I became disillusioned with some of the projects engineers had completed that negatively affect the natural environment: moving rivers into concrete channels, placing bridges, roads, and dams in inappropriate places. All these structures are designed to serve man but have many unintended consequences for the natural environment. For me, a low point was an American Society of Civil Engineers award for a highway project in Orange County, California. In 1993, the San Joaquin Hills Toll Road [SR 73] was constructed. The highway crossed a small stream, Laguna Canyon Creek. This was an exceedingly rare, almost perennial stream in this arid part of the country. The toll road project was huge, and the impact on the stream considerable. During my work for a Californian consulting firm in the late 1970s I had studied this beautiful little creek with vegetated, tree shaded stream banks. Since the time I did the study, not only was the toll road built, but other sections of the creek were put into concrete channels and encroached upon. Perhaps in today's world, the value of this little gem would be recognized, celebrated, and preserved.

I was excited to have a plan to improve the river in front of our camp. On May 29, 1996, I applied for an Inland Lakes and Stream permit from the Michigan Department of Natural Resources to work in the riverine flood plain in front of Boggy's Camp. The photo below shows the Two Hearted River and the eroded bank on the upstream side of our property in 1996. The large red pine in the photo with the exposed roots was completely washed away in the 2010s.

Eroded shoreline and eroded sand bank, looking downstream. Bill Otwell fishing from bank, May 1996.

We did not have the wherewithal to bring in a lot of topsoil, so instead we just asked the MDNR for permission in the permit to install the tree revetments. The idea behind the tree revetments is to lash dead trees along the edge of the river, and then in the spring, sediment will wash down with the high flows and settle out in the water slowed by the tree branches. The strategy behind the revetments is to use normal river processes as it moves sediment downstream and add a little man-induced slowing of the river.

We received the permit and started to lash trees down along the bank with something called a duckbill fastener—an ingenious little device. The fasteners have a duckbill shaped metal piece with a three-foot length of cable attached. The duckbill is driven down into the sand with a metal rod. When the cable is pulled back an inch or two, the duckbill pivots and turns sideways in the hole to secure the cable.

The process is to carry trees brought to the river, and lay them along the bank, trunk upstream. We would find trees with many branches and lots of nooks and crannies to slow water and drop out sediments. We would then locate the end of the duckbill cable we had already placed and wrap a short length of cable around the tree trunk, attaching it to the end of the duckbill. This introduced some small steel cables to the environment, but the idea is that the cable gets covered up as more and more sediments are deposited, creating a stable environment for more vegetation to grow. This both looks and behaves more naturally than a steel sheet pile, concrete walls, or large boulders. These more aggressive forms of protection are not allowed on the banks of a natural river.

We would reconsider the project each summer after the spring flood and add a tree or two. This sounds like a simple endeavor, but I spent hours and hours planning, finding the right tree, and getting help to carry the trees to the river and lash them down. The large jack pines on our property were good candidates after they would die. They were heavy, and only the top portion of the tree was used. The small twigs and needles would create considerable friction in the stream. This technique eventually worked to add material to the toe of the slope.

We also planted trees on the stabilizing slopes. In addition, we maintained steps from the top of the bank to the river that were there when we bought the place. Without these steps, we would have been moving sand towards the river every time we descended.

Tree revetments in place, dogwood growing along stabilized toe of bank.
Looking downstream from in front of Boggy's, 2001.

The stabilized toe of the riverbank was allowing the creation of a shelf of sediments to grow higher. We planted dogwood and willow on this shelf. In the summer, the riverbank was increasingly covered with grass and flowers that were deposited by the river. Butterflies would visit, and an occasional large spider would take up residence.

Trouble was introduced in 2016 when one of the large white pines located in the oxbow upstream of Boggy's broke and fell across the river. This tree was a large 10-foot girth tree that had been leaning towards the river for years. The tree landed with its top on the opposite bank, and the end of its broken trunk on the closer bank, creating a bridge. In the spring of 2017, the annual flood swung the base around until it hit a smaller, white pine on our bank—and in the middle of all of our stream bank protection work.

White pine bridge in the summer of 2017, looking upstream from Boggy's riverbank.

All summer, kayakers and canoers had to get out of their boats and portage around the tree on our riverbank. This created havoc with the work we had done to stabilize the toe of the slope over the past decade. Then the next year, in the spring of 2018, the high flows and the large dead white pine ripped out the smaller white pine, along with a good portion of our stream bank, and they all flowed downstream. The smaller white pine, all its roots, and a portion of our entangled stream bank is still visible in the river downstream of Boggy's. The large white pine amazingly moved about three bends downstream, and we found it stuck up into some live trees on the stream bank. The river demonstrated its power, and we were awed, and discouraged.

CHAPTER 5

THE WATER AND FISH

Hidden Water—Groundwater

Groundwater is the source of the cool, steady base flow into the Two Hearted River that keeps the trout happy all summer. The temperature of groundwater is typically close to the average annual temperature of the region. Groundwater seeping into the Two Hearted River is about 40 degrees Fahrenheit all year long. We can vouch that the Two Hearted is cold in the summer. Even on a summer day, with the sun helping warm the river, it is difficult to enter, and to swim.

Groundwater is also the primary source of drinking water within the Two Hearted River watershed. The amount that precipitation recharges the groundwater in a watershed depends on soil, vegetation, and topography. The groundwater in the Two Hearted River watershed receives a volume of about 15 inches per year spread over the watershed, compared to 32 inches of average total precipitation. The remaining 17 inches of precipitation is lost to evaporation, transpiration, surface runoff, and sublimation.

When we bought our camp, our water supply was provided by an electric pump, located near the river. The pump drew water out of what we thought was a shallow well. We wanted a hand-operated well pump to get rid of the noisy propane generator. In 1992, less than a year after we purchased Boggy's, we installed a two-inch water well over three weekends. The first weekend we used hand augers to bore down to 20 feet, about the level of the river. We had a drive point on the well, and tried pounding the well down into the groundwater, without much luck. A drive point is simply a galvanized well screen that has a sturdy, pointed end. The screen is screwed onto the two-inch well casing. The gravel beds we have in the river in front of Boggy's I think are the layer we ran into. We came back the next weekend with an electric well driver and drove the well to a depth of 40 feet. The third weekend we installed a hand pump. Picture the green hand-pump at a state forest campground. When finished, we poured a small concrete pad around the well. Our kids and dog put their hand and footprints in the wet cement.

When we dismantled the water pump down by the river, we realized what we thought was a shallow well was simply a length of galvanized pipe, connected to a one-inch piece of polyethylene pipe that was in the river. So, we had been drinking untreated river water for a year. It tasted fine and we experienced no sickness. Water from our new groundwater well also tasted great.

Bill Otwell hand driving 2-inch well in 1992.

Water Quality

When initially looking at the Two Hearted River, many folks are surprised that it is amber colored—it looks like tea. The water is clean, and the color is from natural occurring tannins. Tannins come from decomposed organic materials. Hemlock, cedar, and spruce swamps are known to leach amber-colored tannins. When water passes through peaty soils, or other decaying vegetation, it picks up tannins. On a cloudy day, the deep spots in the river can have the appearance of chocolate when seen from a canoe. From the bank, the river normally looks black.

Surveys were taken by the Michigan Department of Environmental Quality, Water Quality Division, at several sites in the watershed in the late 1990s to 2010s to collect data on the macroinvertebrate community, stream habitat, and water chemistry. The "macro" in macroinvertebrates refers to the size of the fauna collected with a net or sieve during the assessments. Macroinvertebrates can include insects, crayfish, snails, clams, worms, leeches, and those of interest to trout anglers like stoneflies, caddisflies, and mayflies. The macroinvertebrates are important because they serve as a link in the food web between the organic matter (leaf litter and algae) and the fish. The stream habitat was characterized as good to excellent, and macroinvertebrates were characterized as acceptable to excellent. No water quality samples exceeded Michigan Water Quality Standards for pollutants.

The Fish of the Two Hearted

The Two Hearted River is a cold-water trout stream. The river is known for steelhead and brook trout fishing. Steelhead are rainbow trout that spend part of their lives in the Great Lakes or the oceans. They are the primary sportfish in the main branch of the Two Hearted River. Some steelhead come into the river in the winter, seeking the warmer groundwater-fed stream, rather than the freezing water of Lake Superior. Most come into the river in the spring, and spawn on gravel beds.

One March we skied in and were outside our camp and heard what sounded like someone bumping into a trashcan. Lo and behold, a flat-bottom aluminum rowboat came around the bend with two anglers. The snow was deep, and the roads not plowed. We could not imagine how the boat got there. It turned out they had towed their boat in behind a snowmobile, launched it at the Reed and Green Bridge, and were going to float the river down to the mouth. Most of the steelhead fishing activity happens in early May. The roads are often unpassable until that time. The weather has warmed, and the mosquitos are not out yet. A wonderful time to be on the river.

Tannins can also affect the color of the fish. My Dad and I caught two nicely sized steelheads in the spring of 1992. My fish was amber colored, like the river, and my dad's was bright silver. We surmised that mine had been in the river a few months, and my dad's had just swum in from Lake Superior, which has crystal-clear water.

The former owner of Boggy's Camp, Jim McCarley, fished mostly for brook trout. He would often not fish the river in front of the camp but would fish the upstream tributaries, small ponds, and lakes in the area. He left us a 1981 Luce County Land Atlas and Plat Book with the brook trout streams and lakes highlighted in yellow. Fishermens' ears perk up when I tell them about this book. I have shown it to a few.

The brook trout (brookies) are Michigan's only native trout and are our state fish. They are beautiful, multicolored wild things. These trout were distributed over eastern North America and the Great Lakes as the glaciers melted. They enjoy cold streams with gravel to lay their eggs. The extensive logging of the watershed in the late 1800s warmed the river by re-moving the shade provided by the trees and introduced sediment that filled the gravel beds. This reduced brook trout populations. The introduction of rainbow trout (steelhead) to the Great Lakes in the late 1800s brought com-petition to their habitat, and further diminished brook trout populations. The mainstream was once an excellent brook trout fishery, all the way to the mouth on Lake Superior. The brook trout lost ground to the steelhead. Now, the South Branch is the best brook trout fishery in the watershed, and some folks think it is one of the best brook trout streams in the state. It is not easy to get to a "brook trout place," but it is a special place to be. An isolated quiet place—clear, crisp waters, often surrounded by tangled trees.

In addition to the brook trout and steelhead, other fish found in the Two Hearted include Menominee whitefish, salmon, brown trout, white and longnose suckers, sculpins, muddlers, and sticklebacks. Some years during the fall, as many as two dozen salmon are observed spawning on the gravel beds in front of our camp. Salmon swimming in the Two Hearted can include coho, Atlantic, pink, and Chinook (king).

The Two Hearted River and its tributaries also support the undesirable Great Lakes invader, the sea lamprey. Sea lampreys have had a negative impact on sport, commercial, and tribal fisheries of the Great Lakes. Sea lampreys are a jawless parasitic fish native to the Atlantic Ocean. Invading the Great Lakes via man-made locks and shipping canals, their aggressive behavior and appetite for fish blood has decimated native fish populations. Sea lampreys were first observed in Lake Ontario in the 1830s. Niagara Falls served as a natural barrier preventing sea lampreys from entering the other Great Lakes, but modifications to the Welland Canal in the early 1900s provided sea lampreys a path to invade the other lakes. In 1921, sea lampreys were first observed in Lake Erie and quickly spread into Lakes Michigan, Huron, and Superior.

The Great Lakes Fishery Commission oversees a Sea Lamprey Management Program for all five Great Lakes, and they contract with the U.S. Fish and Wildlife Service and Fisheries and Oceans Canada to implement an integrated program of sea lamprey control. For the Upper Peninsula, the U.S. Fish and Wildlife Service's Marquette Biological Station oversees sea lamprey control in the Two Hearted River. The Two Hearted was treated with Lampricide in August 2019, and will be monitored and treated as needed in the future.

The banks of the Two Hearted River in front of Boggy's Camp receive a lot of fishing pressure because of great fishing with two gravel beds and easy access. One is directly in front of the cabin (my dad called it the *Honey Hole*), with a second one slightly upstream. John Saxton, the angler we met in the spring of 1991 when we first visited Boggy's Camp, came back yearly in the spring and had been fishing this stretch for 50 years. We often chatted, and I wish I had asked him some more questions, including questions about who Fred "*Boggy*" Young was.

Trout season in Michigan traditionally opens the last Saturday in April. The lower reach of the Two Hearted below County Road 407 (High Bridge) is open year-round for steelhead.

Ed Grunert of Rapid City, South Dakota; Clyde Young and Dick Moore of Caspar, Wyoming; Harold Overholt and Link Fraser of Marquette, and Sherwin Overholt of Sault Ste. Marie spent the past three days fishing at Fred "Boggy" Young's camp, north of Newberry.

The Evening News (**Sault Ste. Marie, Michigan**), **May 28, 1957.**

John Saxton with Claire and a steelhead taken at the Honey Hole in front of Boggy's Camp, spring 1996.

So, as I try to learn more about Boggy Young, it appears that he and his friends were fishing at the camp in 1957. Harold and Sherwin Overholt, Boggy's brothers-in-law, owned the camp at that time.

THE LAND

CHAPTER 6

HISTORY

When one travels north across the eastern Upper Peninsula to reach Boggy's Camp, the dominant view is forest and wetland. Depending on the route, there may be a little settlement here and there, the largest being Newberry with full services. As one leaves Newberry, it may feel like one is approaching the end of civilization in the final 30 miles to Boggy's. Friends who have stayed at our camp have relayed this feeling. The view is forests, a few homes, and a couple of businesses. After crossing the Two Hearted just north of Pine Stump Junction, there are no buildings over the last 10 miles to the cabin. One leaves the paved road and branches off to a gravel road, and the remoteness grows.

The Two Hearted River watershed is found within the boundaries of the Lake Superior State Forest, and is in Northern Luce County in the Upper Peninsula of Michigan. The drainage area is 115,000 acres or 180 square miles. The reason the Two Hearted River is so pure is because of the undeveloped nature of the land. Most damage that comes to any river is from development along its banks, or in the watershed. Rivers would all be pure and clean if we humans would tread more lightly on the land.

The Two Hearted River watershed is north of the much larger Tahquamenon River drainage basin, which flows into Whitefish Bay of Lake

Superior. The watershed is northeast of the Manistique River drainage basin that drains into Lake Michigan. The Fox River flows into the Manistique River.

To shorten the trip between Lakes Superior and Michigan, Indigenous people portaged their canoes between the Tahquamenon and the Fox. The portage was west of present-day Newberry and connected the main branch of the Tahquamenon with the East Branch of the Fox. The portage was one mile long, but it saved them many miles of canoeing through the St. Marys River, and along the shores of Lakes Huron and Michigan.

Covered in Ice

Glaciers covered Michigan until about 35,000 years ago. At that time, the Wisconsin Glacial Stage of the Pleistocene epoch left southern Michigan and started retreating north. The glaciers retreated from the Superior basin only about 10,000 years ago. Lake Algonquin was left behind, which covered most of the Eastern U.P. and all the other Great Lakes. At that time, there was no Two Hearted River.

As the level of Lake Algonquin dropped, the land as we know it today was formed. The Two Hearted and other tributary rivers to Lake Superior served to drain the interior land. Where Boggy's Camp sits, the land to the south across the river is on a higher plateau. This geologic formation is called a "kame." The land drops down the steep bank from this plateau to the river valley, then climbs out from the river northerly to the top of the bank on our property.

The topography then gradually drops to the north, all the way to Lake Superior. When Lake Algonquin retreated, a series of small sand dunes were formed. Lake Nipissing was a glacial lake that came after Lake Algonquin and may have been the final stage where the dunes north of the camp were formed. One unique feature of the dunes is that they all run east-west. When we are out wandering in the woods towards the big lake, it is easy to get turned around on a cloudy day. The regular pattern of the small dunes keeps us oriented and heading north.

A small portion of our little two-acre parcel is in the Two Hearted River drainage basin, but everything sloping to the north is in the Lake Superior basin. From our camp, the river meanders east for about 5 miles as the crow flies, or 10 river miles. I expect as the land drained the melting glacier, the incipient river found an east/west valley, sloping to the east, and the water cut through the glacial materials until it reached Lake Superior.

Wearing my engineering hard hat, I have conducted many hydrogeological investigations in Northern Michigan and the U.P. These investigations include sampling and characterizing subsurface soils with the use of drill rigs. The work was completed either to look for groundwater to supply community drinking water, or to determine if soil or groundwater contamination had occurred. If there is contamination, the goal is to track the extent in subsurface soils, and in the ground water.

No one was here when the glaciers were retreating, so we do not know exactly how the glaciers dropped the glacial materials, and how they were then moved and sorted with the melt water. When drilling near downtown Traverse City, the soils are homogeneous beach sands, with the groundwater table a reflection of the height of Grand Traverse Bay. In other places, the glacial till is a mixed-up mess of stones, sand, clay, and silt, difficult to characterize and assess. The only soil boring I have done near our camp was a 20-foot-deep hand auger boring for our own well. Based on this boring, the soil under Boggy's Camp is sand and gravel.

The View from Boggy's Camp, 4,000 years ago

The glaciers are gone, Lake Nipissing retreating, the general shape of the river valley is established. The Two Hearted River continues to cut its course through the glacial materials and extends its headwaters upstream. The advancement of the glaciers pushed the forests south. The forests are now returning north. Animals, although some could easily move north (deer, moose, etc.), would not have moved north until the vegetation they rely on would be available. Predators (mountain lion, wolf, etc.) also would not have moved north until their prey had returned.

Native Americans and the European Invasion

Indigenous people resided in this part of Michigan since the glaciers retreated. Stone tools found in the western U.P. show native tribes present for about the past 8,000 years. Because of the lingering glacial lakes covering the low and flat eastern U.P., people moved in later.

The Anishinabek (the real, or original people), spoke Anishinaabemowin. Legend has it that the Ojibwe (Chippewa), the Odawa (Ottawa), and the Bodewadmi (Potawatomi) all travelled west from the Atlantic Ocean. They canoed up the St. Lawrence and Ottawa rivers, into the Mattawa River to Lake Nipissing, then through the French River into Lake Huron. The three tribes of the Anishinabek then went their own way. The Ojibwe went north and followed the St. Marys River to the rapids at what is now Sault Ste. Marie. Reports from French missionaries in the mid 1600s observed up to 2,000 Native Americans camped by the rapids each October for the whitefish harvest. Estimates were that 200 permanent residents resided at the rapids year round; the rest were seasonal visitors. The visitors then broke up into smaller family units and moved to other villages for the winter, spring, and summer. *Hinsdale's Archaeological atlas of Michigan* describes a Native American village at the mouth of the Two Hearted, a burial ground just to the west of it. The 1973 Natural River Plan suggested that an archaeological survey of the Two Hearted River would reveal numerous prehistoric Native American archaeological sites. I could not find evidence of such a survey.

The Michigan Territory was created in 1805. Territorial Governor Lewis Cass negotiated an agreement with the Ojibwe in 1820 (Treaty of Sault Ste. Marie). The treaty allowed the Americans to build a fort on the St. Marys River to guard the entrance to Lake Superior. The Ojibwe ceded 10,000 acres of land on the banks of the river. The treaty allowed the Ojibwe to still fish and camp on that land.

In 1836, the Odawa and the Ojibwe ceded 10 million acres to the U.S. government—the Treaty of Washington. This land included the northern part of the Lower Peninsula, and the eastern half of the Upper Peninsula. Compensation the two tribes received included $600,000, to be paid over 20 years, along with some additional funds to be used to pay off debts to the fur traders, and pay for education, farming implements, and medicine. The ownership of 250,000 acres of land was also part of the deal. The U.S. Senate then amended the agreement to a five-year period, hoping to force the displacement of the Native Americans to the west. By 1850, the U.S. was no longer trying to move the tribes to western prairies. In 1855, the Ojibwe signed the Treaty of Detroit. This treaty preserved land from public sale for the benefit of the Ojibwe. Chiefs who participated in this treaty represented people who lived on the south shore of Lake Superior from

Grand Island east to Sault Ste. Marie and then down the St. Marys River to Drummond Island.

The land allotment was not successful. The Indigenous people did not view land ownership the same way that the Europeans did. Much of the land in the eastern U.P. has poor soils and a short growing season, so farming was difficult. Some of the land specifically set aside for the Native tribes had already been secured by land speculators. It is hardly fair, trading 10 million acres for 250,000 acres, many of which were not secured by the Native Americans. In addition, did the Indigenous folks really want money to pay for modern medicine and our education system?

There is currently a movement in the United States to reclaim former Indigenous land. Called "land back," some of these efforts include buying former tribal land on the open market. In 2020, Congress voted to restore ownership of 19,000 acres of the national bison range in Montana to native tribes.

The View from Boggy's Camp, 1885

Can you imagine how beautiful the river was back then? Huge white pine trees. No roads. The rolling sand hills bordering the river would have been full of mature forests, instead of the clear-cuts and jack pine plantations that one sees now. A group of four large white pines would be growing in the oxbow island upstream of Boggy's. Wolf, bear, moose, and mountain lion would have been wandering the woods. Woodland caribou were still in the watershed. Steelhead had not been introduced into the Great Lakes, and native brook trout were thriving. Fred "Boggy" Young was born this year in Southampton, England.

Michigan—a State Is Born

The first European to set eyes on Lake Superior may have been the French explorer Étienne Brûlé in 1622. He was the first White person in Ontario and the first to visit Lakes Ontario, Huron, and Superior. The French Jesuit missionary Claude-Jean Allouez sailed around the lake and mapped it in 1667.

French fur trading then flourished, but the entire region came under British control in the late 1700s. Control of trade remained in the hands of the British until 1817, when John Jacob Astor and his American Fur Company took over the trade south of the Canadian border. This company flourished on the back of the beaver, and the backs of the Native Americans trained to trap the beaver. The beaver was wiped out throughout most of the northern United States and Canada.

Michigan became a state in 1837. The state had all the township corners in the Upper Peninsula surveyed in the 1840s. In the 1850s, surveyors went back and surveyed the corners of the 36 sections in each township. Before these surveys, there was no way to describe property boundaries, except geographic boundaries like rivers. After the survey, property could be described according to section, township, and range. In Michigan, this system extends from ground zero just south of Lansing.

A line that extends east-west along the south edge of Ingham County all the way across the State of Michigan is the Base Line, and all the townships in Michigan are numbered consecutively north or south of this line. Another line is drawn north-south through the middle of Ingham County. This is the Meridian Line and extends all the way north to and through the U.P. Townships are numbered consecutively east or west of this line. Townships were surveyed and are typically 36 square miles, or 6 miles by 6 miles square. There are over 1,000 townships in Michigan. Political townships can be larger, and McMillan Township, where the Two Hearted watershed is located, contains a total of 604 square miles. McMillan Township is the largest municipality by acreage in Michigan.

In the 1840s, iron ore was discovered in the central U.P., and copper on the U.P.'s Keweenaw Peninsula. These discoveries attracted both immigrants and Americans to the U.P. The first Euro-American report I found that mentioned travelling up the Two Hearted River was from *The Autobiography of Captain Alexander McDougall*. In 1875, the captain learned his ship would not be needed until July 1 because there was nothing to haul. He went to Sault Ste. Marie, rented a small rowboat, and put that on a ship that dropped him off near the mouth of the "Two Hart Rivers." From the McDougall autobiography:

> *In those days, there were only a few huts on the 175 miles of shoreline. I found here at the mouth the greatest lot of large brook trout I ever saw, hundreds of*

them, four, five, and six-pound trout catching minnows coming out of the river. I caught quickly a lot of them and put them in a pen made of boulder rocks. Then I went up the river, exploring a supposed coal formation, and found it to be only a streak of hard peat or lignite coal. It might have been a good idea to drill there for coal at a greater depth, and I now think it possible some good deposits of coal or oil exist in the great empty section of flat lands.

When I came away, I brought with me about 100 pounds of trout and rowed out to catch a cargo steamer at dusk, but the crew paid no attention to my signals and, with the wind offshore, I pulled on my oars all night against a head wind, reaching White Fish Point about 8:00 am. The lighthouse keeper came out and found me asleep on the sand beach, entirely played out.

Boggy's little two-acre parcel is in Section 11, Township 49 North, Range 10 West. The ownership of the property has changed regularly since it was first surveyed. After the glaciers left, the landscape was fresh and untrammeled. The flora and fauna came back with time, and eventually Native Americans visited the watershed on a seasonal basis. After the surveys, the land originally owned by the U.S. Government was transferred to private individuals, many of them associated with logging companies.

In a plat book dated 1927–1936, Cleveland-Cliffs owned 400 acres in our Section 11, and private individuals owned 240 acres. Cleveland-Cliffs, discussed later in the book, was an early mining company that owned land across the U.P. In a 1930 plat book, the U.S. Government owned 200 acres, the Michigan Forest Reserve owned 120 acres, and private ownership was 320 acres. In 1981, the State of Michigan owned 576 acres, with 62 acres in private ownership (the 2 are our Boggy's Camp property). In 2022, the 62 acres in private ownership had all changed hands since the 1981 book; the rest of the section ownership was unchanged.

It is apparent that Harry Young obtained 80 acres in Section 11 by taxes paid in 1918. Harry was Fred (Boggy) Young's father. This land was southwest of Boggy's and not on the river. This property had originally been obtained from the U.S. Government in 1890. In 1936, Harry sold this land to his son, Boggy, and then Boggy transferred it to the state in 1939. In 1944, Boggy transferred an additional 20 acres to the state. This parcel was also not on the river but was located just north of Boggy's Camp.

For this transfer, Boggy received the two-acre parcel on the river we own today. Convoluted for sure—we do not know the why, who, or what for—but I am glad it all worked out. The Youngs must have had friends in the right places.

CHAPTER 7

FORESTRY AND LOGGING

When Laura and I visited our camp in October 2022, we heard equipment across the river, on the high bank just south of our camp. The logging noise seemed close, and the activity went on for about a week. When a large tree was felled, we could feel the ground shake. We felt anxious and invaded—normally we enjoy a peaceful, quiet view of the forests on the high bank across the river. Our state forest neighbor across the river seemed to have been transformed into an industrial site.

On a quiet Sunday we walked down to the Reed and Green Bridge, then backtracked on CR 410 to check on the results of the logging. A large swath of forest had been cut, selectively. There were large stacks of conifer logs and a stack of white birch. We were pleased to see some larger white pines still standing, along with some maples. The required 100-foot minimum buffer between the logging and the Two Hearted River seemed to have been honored.

The logs left the watershed and headed into the mills for processing. Jobs were produced ranging from forest management to the logging, from the truck drivers to the mill workers. The impact on Boggy's Camp was minimal. The impact on Laura and me? It just added fuel to our reflections on the consequences of progress. The forest will recover, hopefully in a sustainable, resilient way. Animal residents of this section of land were affected, some greatly. Fungi, which play such a key role in forest ecology as described later in this chapter, were also affected in a negative way.

Glaciers have pushed northern species of plants and animals farther and farther south as the glaciers advanced. The process of glaciation took thousands of years and had been repeated several times over the past million years. After each glacier retreat, the forest moved back north following the retreating ice. After getting scraped by the glacier, vegetation returned, first the lichen, then moss, then grasses. Shrubs followed, and then the first trees. Disturbances such as clear-cut logging and fires also result in reforestation. The returning forest is dependent on what survived the disturbance, along with climate, soil type, and moisture.

Trappers, surveyors, and other early explorers of the north woods reported huge stands of white pines. Landowners and logging companies hired timber cruisers to quantify potential sales. These folks were trained in measuring forest characteristics important to determine economic value. Cruisers would estimate average tree size, volume, species, and quality. The purpose of this data was for lumber companies to then put in bids for certain stands.

Laura was employed as a timber cruiser for the U.S. Forest Service as a summer intern in 1978. She was a student at Michigan State University, thinking of going into the Forestry Program. She worked in South Dakota in the Black Hills National Forest. She was marking trees in preparation for logging. Laura talks of this experience with fond memories. *"Being able to walk and wander through majestic stands of Ponderosa Pine all day was not a hardship."*

After the cruisers quantified the value of the woods, the harvest of the virgin white pines started. Human power of many men and horsepower did the harvesting. Crosscut saws, cant hooks, pickaroons, splitting mauls, axes, and wedges were some tools of the trade. Cant hooks were used to roll and lift logs. A pickaroon was also used to move logs by hand.

Logging in the U.P. occurred in three general periods:

1. The Pine, Muscle, and Water period from the 1870s to 1900. The large white pines were cut down by human power and moved by horses and water.

Logging tools exhibit on the side of Tahquamenon Logging Museum in Newberry.

2. The Hardwood, Steam Engine, and Rail period from 1890 to the 1930s. Steam-powered railroads were common by that time to move the logs.

3. And the third, Pulpwood and Petroleum, which started in the 1930s and continues today.

Pine, Muscle, and Water

Three colorful pine logging men dominated the Two Hearted watershed: George Dawson, Robert Dollar, and Con Culhane. They left their marks and their names. Because log transport originally was mostly by water, logging in the Lake Superior watershed didn't get really going until the first canal was built around the St. Marys River rapids at Sault Ste. Marie in the mid-1850s. Also, at that time, an agreement was made between the British North American provinces (now Canada) and the United States. This trade agreement allowed natural products like lumber to move easily between the two countries. The British/Canadians had a demand for long, squared timber for ship masts in England, where large trees were gone. The French-Canadians had the skills to square them off.

George Dawson was born in Kingston, Ontario, in 1839, and died in

Sault Ste. Marie in 1894. Dawson started logging the U.P. in the 1860s. His expertise and the market he sought was for squared timbers. There were many concerns about this practice because it wasted so much of the tree. The lower trunk, the sides, the branches, and the top were all wasted. Dawson oversaw logging camps from Grand Marais to the Sault, concentrating along the Two Hearted River. His loggers spent the fall through early winter cutting and shaping the pine. Most of his crew would then leave, and a smaller crew would continue shaping, and then float the logs in the spring to Lake Superior.

Captain Robert Dollar was born in Scotland in 1844. He immigrated with his father to Canada in 1858. As a youth he worked as a helper in a Canadian lumber camp and then in 1866 became a foreman. In 1871, he bought his first piece of forest. He moved to Michigan and continued his rise in the logging industry.

Dollar bought land from the Detroit, Mackinac and Marquette Railroad (DMMRR), and started a mill on the Tahquamenon River, just west of Newberry. As an incentive to get the railroad built, a land grant of 1.3 million acres of U.P. forests had been approved by the Michigan legislature and given to the railroad. Only 40 years after Michigan became a state, and the U.P. forests were first surveyed, these lands were given to a railroad by the new state. These same lands had been occupied by Indigenous people for thousands of years. Looking back on this, it seems wrong and unjust.

The railroad, completed in 1881, stretched from Marquette to St. Ignace. The DMMRR allowed Dollar to live in Marquette and attend to his business near Newberry. He used the railroad for travel, so he could supervise workers on the Tahquamenon, Two Hearted, Au Train, and Laughing Whitefish Rivers. He used these rivers to move his logs to Lake Superior. Dollar would then raft them to Saginaw Bay for processing.

In the late 1880s, Dollar grew tired of the U.P. winters and moved to California. There he got involved in shipping. He was successful, and he built an 11-story office building in San Francisco in 1911, which was the headquarters of the Dollar Steamship Company. In 1928, he made the cover of *Time* magazine. Dollar died in San Francisco, California, in 1932.

Born in Ireland in 1840, Con Culhane started logging in the Two Hearted watershed around 1890 and continued until 1903. When he arrived in the U.P., many of the easy-to-access large pines were gone. He went after the more difficult-to-reach trees, for example, those in the low area between the Two Hearted and Tahquamenon Rivers. He bought a steam locomotive from southern Michigan, and named it after his wife, the "Ellen K." He would lay out his own railroads, log the area, pull up the tracks, and move them to the next area. Here is more on Culhane from a 1978 article by noted U.P. writer and historian Dixie Franklin:

> To hear lumberjacks tell it, Con Culhane had Paul Bunyan beat all to heck.
>
> Legends grew fast as saws downed the white pines along the Tahquamenon River between 1880 and 1903. Tales of Culhane's flying fists and his puffing trains spread long after he was run over by one of his own steam engines . . .
>
> Around 1890, he brought his wife Ellen and son Billy to the logging country around the Little Two Hearted River. He went to work on a tract of land. . . He built a sluice dam and log pond and had a raft of logs ready in hours, heading into Lake Superior, bound for Muskegon.
>
> The "beautiful lady," as he called 'Ma' Culhane, said that was good, but Con could do better. By then, the timber cut was a long way back from the river. What Con needed was a railroad . . .
>
> He laid rails in two-mile sections across the bog and muskeg. Driving the locomotives to the end of the line, he picked up the rails behind him and laid them in the front all the way to the Tahquamenon above the falls.
>
> Across the river, Culhane built Ma another White House, as he did in all his camps. He always kept his "beautiful lady" in fine style.
>
> The well-educated woman didn't mind his swashbuckling ways and often held the lantern as he tied into his rollicking, free-for-all, no-holds-barred fights. As boss, he felt it his bound duty to lick every man in camp. Besides, it was their only entertainment.

On June 26, 1903, Culhane was riding on one of his train cars and stepped across the top of the cars to talk to the brakeman. The engineer slowed down to unhook some cars. The train jerked, and Culhane fell between the cars. He was crushed and killed instantly.

All three of the above men have geographic features named after them: Dawson Creek, a major tributary in the Two Hearted River system; Dollarville, a once thriving village on the Tahquamenon River, just west of

Newberry; and Culhane Lake, near Lake Superior, just east of the Two Hearted River watershed.

Water was the primary means to move the white pine logs. White pine was also known as "cork pine" because it was so buoyant. The large white pine logs were logged close to Lake Superior, and then sent up the Two Hearted River and other rivers for convenient access. Short haul roads were built for horses to drag sleds full of logs in the winter to the river, or Lake Superior. The haul roads were sometimes coated with ice to help the sleds. In the spring, the logs were floated down the river.

Several water control structures were placed along the Two Hearted River to help float logs during the spring log drives in the late 1800s. These structures have been mentioned in reports and labelled on various historical maps. One former structure was the Spile Dam on the West Branch, about one-half mile upstream from its confluence with the main branch. Another was the Hemlock Dam, located south of the existing CCI road on the South Branch, and then another Spile Dam on the East Branch.

"Spile Dam" is a common name for simple structures made of timbers. I have found no evidence any of these structures still exist. In October 2022, Laura and I trekked upstream following the West Branch to the reported former site of the Spile Dam. We believe we found the narrow point in the valley where a dam could be efficiently located, but there was no evidence of a past structure. A beaver dam was located just upstream. A furry engineer also thought the location a good one to pool water, albeit for non-economic reasons.

In Michigan, navigable streams are defined as those that floated logs during the lumbering days. The so-called "Floating Log" test has been through many court battles because navigable streams allow public access. Not all wealthy riparian owners want to share their water with the public.

Most of the structures associated with the logging camps are also gone. There were many small, temporary camps. The equipment and some of the timbers would be moved to set up a new camp as sections of the forest were cleared out. Some of the cabins at the East Branch Sportsmen's Club (EBSC) were part of a former lumber camp on the property. EBSC is a fishing and hunting club that started in the 1930s and still has members today.

Hardwood, Steam Engine, and Rail

As the pine forests dwindled, attention was focused on the hardwood forests. Hardwood does not float like pine, so different techniques were necessary to move the logs. Also, larger companies came in to replace the many smaller logging companies. These companies had the resources to build railroads to move their trees, and funds to build larger lumber mills and furnaces that were needed to process hardwoods.

Large firms, like the Cleveland-Cliffs Iron Company, took a sophisticated approach to forest management. Cleveland-Cliffs was formed in 1891, when the Cleveland Iron Mining Company (CIMC) purchased the Iron Cliffs Company. The CIMC was formed in 1847 by some businesspeople from Cleveland, Ohio. They shipped their first load of U.P. iron ore to Cleveland in 1855. This was the year the first Soo Lock opened on the St. Marys River at Sault Ste. Marie. One of the early challenges for the CIMC was how to make a profit in a very isolated place. The wilds of the U.P. must have been both scary and enchanting to the folks from urbanizing Cleveland. They got over these fears due to the lure of potential profits.

Samuel Livingston Mather was one of these Ohioans who moved north. He was an officer, and then president of CIMC from 1853 until he died in 1890. His son, William G. Mather, had started working at CIMC in 1878. William became president of CIMC when his father died and then president of the combined Cleveland-Cliffs from 1891 to 1933. Mathers were in charge for 80 years! Cleveland-Cliffs began diversifying in the 1890s to control more of the natural resources they needed to produce iron, and to develop new profit centers. In 1901, Cleveland-Cliffs purchased a million acres from the Detroit, Mackinac and Marquette Railroad. Cleveland-Cliffs, at its peak in the early 1900s, owned 1.5 million acres of land in the U.P. They were one of the largest forest owners in the U.S. They purchased this land to provide wood to run the blast furnaces that they were building. The first furnace was built in Gladstone, then one in Marquette and then Carp River. The primary purpose of the blast furnaces was to make pig iron from the iron ore mined in the western U.P.

In 1901, William Mather bought most of Grand Island in Lake Superior. The island is just north of the town of Munising and west of Pictured Rocks National Lakeshore. The island is now part of the Hiawatha National Forest. A National Forest display on the island in 2022 stated that:

Mather shared some of the conservation ideas of Progressive Era leaders like Teddy Roosevelt. He preserved ancient forests and repaired historic Fur Trade Era buildings.

There was also a 1908 *Detroit News-Tribune* referred to:

On this Great Island, which represents the soul of a modern corporation, the birds and beasts run wild . . . no stick of timber has ever crossed the channel from the island to be used in the pursuit of the almighty dollar.

William Mather died in 1951, and that year Cleveland-Cliffs started harvesting the large trees on the island. Laura and I took a ferry to Grand Island in October 2022. We rented a cabin for two nights and spent a day riding mountain bikes around the island. The trail was the old rim road. There were gorgeous views from on top of limestone cliffs, not unlike Pictured Rocks National Lakeshore. The Mather Cabin still stands on the west side of the island.

Mather Cabin, Grand Island.

In 1903, Cleveland-Cliffs added a forestry graduate from Cornell University, one of the first companies to have a full-time forester. They practiced selective cutting and looked at the forest from the perspective of preserving their land holdings for decades. They also had patrols that would try to keep an eye out for forest fires. Eventually, Cleveland-Cliffs moved towards clear cutting to feed their hungry lumber mills. These mills had to have different streams of production because of the various products that they now made from hardwood. These included barrels, flooring, furniture, paneling, and cordwood for charcoal.

Pulpwood and Petroleum

The third phase of lumbering, which continues today, uses diesel-powered equipment to log and move the timber to the mills. By the 1930s, there was less private ownership of the forests, and more forestland owned by the state and federal government. More emphasis was put on managing the forests to allow for future harvest.

Although petroleum-powered vehicles with internal combustion engines became common by the 1920s, they were not commonly used to move logs until the 1940s. The early trucks were not very sturdy, were prone to breakdown, and had trouble negotiating the newly cut two-tracks in the forests. Horses still ruled.

Today, industrial scale harvesting looks vastly different from the early years. Giant harvesters can cut the tree, delimb the trunk, and cut the trunk up to specified lengths. A second machine will come in, pick up the cut logs, and load them onto trucks to haul to the mills. Petroleum intensive, man-power light.

This was the logging that was going on across the river from our camp that week in October 2022. The area cut was about 40 acres. Two men, two machines, and trucks picking up the logs.

CHAPTER 8

TODAY'S FOREST

And into the forest I go, to lose my mind and find my soul.

—John Muir

Lake Superior State Forest

The US Army built the first lumber mill in the U.P. in Sault Ste. Marie in 1822 to help build Fort Brady. Logging of white pine started statewide in the 1830s and peaked around 1900. An independent Forestry Commission was established in Michigan in 1887. The Forestry Commission was established because of growing public concern about wasteful logging practices and forest fires in the logged-over land. Surprisingly, there was concern noted even back then about logging's impact on water resources. Professor William Beal of the Michigan Agricultural College wrote in the late 1800s, *"To the best of my knowledge, lumbering has always been overdone in this state."*

Professor Beal was considered the father of Michigan forestry. In 1875 he did an experimental planting of 150 distinct species of trees on the college's campus. He then wrote the first experiment station study on forestry in 1886, *Lessons on Growing Forest Trees*. Many of these trees, planted out in front of the MSU Union in East Lansing, are beautiful, large specimens today.

Public officials also began to realize that some land should be retained in public ownership. Much of the logged-over land was considered worthless by its owners and reverted to state ownership due to nonpayment of taxes, especially in the northern part of the state and the U.P. Fires were a continuing concern because of the abandoned land. In 1871, fires burned two million acres in the central lower peninsula, and in 1881, fires burned one million acres in the "thumb" of Michigan.

The first forest reserves became the Higgins Lake and Houghton Lake State Forests and were dedicated in 1904. These areas included 34,000 acres of tax reverted land. Trees were purchased from commercial dealers and planted to begin the reforestation. The first Forest Reserve Manual outlined the following goals in the early 1900s according to a 2014 MSU Extension article.

1. *To protect and improve the forest cover and thereby produce a crop of timber on lands which are largely unsuited to other kinds of crops.*
2. *To encourage settlement by lessening the dangers from fire and by restoring to the land the attractive and useful cover.*
3. *To encourage by direct help and good example, better protection of private lands.*
4. *To regulate the use of these lands and such materials as they now offer, especially to regulate the grazing upon these lands to avoid useless, destructive overgrazing.*
5. *To assure to the county and town at least some return in place of regular taxes. The law now provides that the State through its Forestry Commission may contribute to the maintenance of roads and schools in the towns where the Forest Reserves are located.*
6. *To furnish employment in the protection and care of the forests.*

There is no mention of wildlife, water quality, or protection of the ecosystem in these goals. Some of the Two Hearted River watershed became part of the Lake Superior State Forest in 1913, one of Michigan's first state forests. There were 600,000 acres under state ownership in 1916, and seven state forests, including the Lake Superior State Forest. State forest officers were charged with tree planting and fire protection. The University of Michigan started adding classes in forestry in 1881, the first university in the country to do so. In 1902, Michigan Agricultural College (now Michigan State University) established a Forestry Department, The University of Michigan in 1903, and Michigan Technological University in 1936. The state forest system grew from 34,000 acres in 1904 to about 4 million acres in 2000.

The goals of the original Forest Reserve Manual took time to achieve. A January 1921 *New York Times* article titled, "A Third of Michigan a Waste and Poor," described Michigan's fall from forest leadership:

> *A third of Michigan virtually is bankrupt, is unable to pay its way with schools and roads and is getting poorer instead of richer from year to year, according to P.S. Lovejoy of the Forestry Faculty of the University of Michigan. While the world suffers from a shortage of forest products, millions of acres of Michigan land which once yielded vast wealth in timber are today waste lands, fire swept and deteriorating year by year . . .*
>
> *The third of Michigan referred to by Lovejoy, covers 10,000,000 acres or so, the most of it being in the northern part of the Lower Peninsula, the rest in the Upper Peninsula. The bulk of these bankrupt lands were originally pine forests. From 1870 to 1900 Michigan led the world in the quality, quantity and value of its timber exports. Today, that State is a tremendous importer of timber and other forest products . . .*
>
> *The hickory for the wheels of Michigan automobiles is coming from Arkansas and Mississippi. The oak for Grand Rapids furniture is being cut in Louisiana and Tennessee. Michigan does not even supply herself with enough telephone poles and railroad ties, but imports poles from Idaho, and ties from Virginia.*

Between 1921 and 1932, two million tax delinquent acres were added to the state forest system. In 1933, as part of the New Deal, the federal government established the Civilian Conservation Corps (CCC) camps, which went a long way towards reforesting Northern Michigan. These camps were involved in planting trees and fire control, including constructing fire access lanes. By 1934, there were 13 camps with about 200 men in each camp located on state land in the U.P. A tribute on County Road 410 on our way into Boggy's marks a location of one of the former CCC camps. The vast red pine plantations started by the CCC are still evident across Northern Michigan and the U.P.

Former Perch Lake CCC location on County Road 410.

Since 2006, state forests have become certified by third-party auditors. Two organizations, the Forest Stewardship Council (FSC) and the Sustainable Forestry Initiative (SFI), aim to support responsible and sustainable management of state and private forests. The organizations audit the MDNR's management practices with respect to social, economic, and biological standards. The evolving standards of these two organizations work to improve forest management while protecting the environment. The certification process intends for these forests to continue to provide economic and social benefits.

According to the MDNR, as of December 2020, these programs certified four million acres of state forest. In addition, two million acres of private forest were certified by the two programs combined.

The MDNR produces a State Forest Plan which provides a detailed assessment of forestry plans for different regions, which are updated every 10 years. Sustainability goals include growing more volume of lumber on state land than the MDNR cuts or thins each year. The Two Hearted watershed is in the Eastern Upper Peninsula plan. Specifically, three of the 31 management areas in the Eastern U.P. contain parts of the Two Hearted watershed: 1) Deer Park, 2) Two Hearted Headwaters, and 3) Tahqua-menon River Patterned Fen. For each management area, detailed analyses for subareas include considering forest cover type, featured wildlife spe-cies—including any rare species and special resource areas (e.g., old growth, patterned fen)—forest health (pests and invasive species), fire management, public access and recreation (campgrounds, hunting, canoeing), and water resources management. This is a much more comprehensive management analysis than the early state forest plans.

The Deer Park management area is 92,000 acres. This rectangular area extends from the Alger County line east along Lake Superior to the mouth of the Two Hearted and beyond to east of the Little Two Hearted River. The rectangular area extends south to the North Branch of the Two Hearted. Much of the north portion of this management area is outside the Two Hearted River watershed.

The Two Hearted Headwaters management area is 18,000 acres, and lies south of the Deer Park management area and west of County Road 407. State land is intermixed with Nature Conservancy lands. The headwa-ters of the North Branch, West Branch, South Branch, and Dawson Creek are all in this area. In addition, the Pretty Lakes Complex is located here.

The Tahquamenon River Patterned Fen management area is 30,000 acres, and is located east of County Road 407, and southeast of the Head-waters management area. This area lies in both the Two Hearted and Tahquamenon watersheds and contains the largest contiguous expanse of wetlands in the state. These wetlands lie on a sandy glacial lake plain. The McMahon Lake and Sleeper Lake Patterned Fens are in this area, as well as the headwaters of the East Branch and a tributary of Dawson Creek.

A Friend to the Watershed—the Nature Conservancy

We do not inherit the earth from our ancestors, we borrow it from our children.
                                                              —Dennis J. Hall

Our family visited one of the Nature Conservancy preserves in the early 1990s. We enjoyed the wilderness hike into McMahon Lake, saw moose tracks and not another hiker. I contacted TNC and wondered whether I could volunteer some time. We discussed the idea of putting some monitor wells in the patterned fen to determine the direction of groundwater flow, the slope of the water table, and obtain water samples. The wells would allow for future sampling and monitoring.

In July 1994, I met TNC staff Dave Ewert and intern Libby, along with local volunteers John Allen and Teddy Maynard. We hiked into McMahon Lake and spent time circumnavigating the fen. I worked up a plan to install some hand-driven monitor wells. After subsequent discussions, it was determined not to install the wells. Part of the consideration was that TNC owned much of the fen, so it was protected from outside influence.

The Nature Conservancy (TNC) has had extraordinary involvement in the Two Hearted watershed over the past several decades. Why the focus of their scientists and fundraisers on this little watershed? TNC started in 1950 when an established organization, the Ecologists Union, changed its name to the Nature Conservancy. TNC purchased its first parcel, a 60-acre hemlock forest in Bedford, New York, in 1955. By the 1980s, TNC had evolved to consider larger tracts of land, what they term "ecoregional planning." The Two Hearted River watershed got on TNC's radar because of the wonderful natural features; considerable quantities of rare, threatened, and endangered species; limited access by people; and a manageable size. The Two Hearted watershed presented an unusual opportunity to protect a substantial proportion of a basically intact and undeveloped watershed.

Starting with a 1,000-acre gift, TNC established the McMahon Lake Preserve in 1989. After additional gifts, the preserve now sits at 4,000 acres, and is in the headwaters of the East Branch of the Two Hearted River. This preserve contains McMahon Lake, along with a patterned fen, a rare type of peat bog. A patterned fen is a wetland with a series of peat ridges and troughs (strings and flarks). These features are perpendicular to the flow of groundwater. The saturated troughs of the fens have sphagnum mosses and sedges, whereas the ridges have shrubs and scattered small, stunted trees. The McMahon Patterned Fen spans over 5,000 acres, one of the largest in Michigan. In Michigan, patterned fens are currently imperiled. The fens are found only in the boreal and sub-boreal regions of North America, Europe, and Siberia. In Michigan, they occur only in the eastern U.P.

The Nature Conservancy worked in the early 2000s to establish the 23,000-acre Two Hearted River Forest Reserve. The reserve allows logging, but on a very controlled basis. The second-growth forest has smaller trees,

Aerial photo of McMahon Lake and the Patterned Fen. *From Google*

and few tree species. The goal of the reserve is to thin some trees to help the forest attain old-growth characteristics more quickly than if the forest was left alone. The current forest lacks habitat suitable for diverse flora and fauna. Selling the trees harvested also helps provide funds for additional conservation projects and provides local jobs.

Some TNC forests in the southwest portion of the watershed are dominated by sugar maple. TNC partnered with Michigan-based Connor Sports, the NCAA's official basketball court supplier, to provide maple for a Final-Four floor. The Final Four are the final four teams in the annual Division I college basketball championships. This allowed Connor to follow the maple from one source to their mill, which is also in the U.P.

TNC produced a video on the Two Hearted project titled *A Good Cut: Restoring the Forests of Michigan's Upper Peninsula*. TNC's consulting forester John Fosgitt was interviewed:

> *The relationship between the Nature Conservancy and foresters in Michigan's Upper Peninsula is a very unique one. Most people don't think of the Nature Conservancy as cutting timber. They think of the Nature Conservancy as someone that is protecting timber. . . .*
>
> *By embracing the idea of working forests and sustainable forestry, we're able to prove that you can have an ecological benefit as well as continuing to provide jobs in timber to the economy. . . .*

They [forests] *serve to buffer the watersheds and water quality and clean air. But they're just as important and part of the fabric of who the people of the Upper Peninsula are. . . .*

The reserve allows hunting, fishing, and trapping, but access is limited to hiking or cross-country skiing. Automobiles, off-road vehicles (ORVs), motorcycles, snowmobiles, and even bicycles are prohibited. TNC does allow an existing snowmobile trail to continue to cross the property. The deep snowpack helps to protect the vegetation and soils from damage. This trail that traverses the reserve property, known as the CCI road, also allows motorized vehicles the rest of the year.

This reserve was part of an even larger "Big U.P. Deal" that created a 270,000-acre conservation easement in 2005, described as the largest land deal in Michigan history. The corporation Great Lakes Forest 1 owns much of the working forest conservation easement land adjacent to TNC property. The Kamehameha Schools Trust of Hawaii owned the land and sold it in 2002. The trust was a financial partner with Benson Forests, who left the project in 1994.

Most of this land had previously been owned by the Cleveland-Cliffs Iron Company. Cleveland-Cliffs sold 292,000 acres of land to Benson and Kamehameha in 1991. Ben Benson and his partner owned the property for several years and created controversary in the U.P. A July 27, 1993, article in the *Detroit Free Press* lays out the battle: "*A New Overlord—Land czar fencing with Yoopers.*" U.P. residents (Yoopers) had concerns with long fences on two of his Lake Superior coastal residential developments. Yoopers do not like fences, or out-of-town developers.

In the first two years Benson owned the U.P. property, he sold 1,274 acres to individuals for development. About 70 acres of that land was located on Lake Superior, just north of Boggy's Camp. That property, with 1,320 feet on Lake Superior, has been divided up into ten lots. Five cabins have been built. Benson Forests also sold over 500 acres to expand Pictured Rocks National Lakeshore, and over 2,200 acres to the state for Tahquamenon Falls State Park.

The "Big U.P." conservation easement allows continued public access with restrictions, along with limits on development rights. The easement will prevent land fragmentation. The Michigan Natural Resources Trust

Fund, the Federal Forest Legacy program, the Charles Stewart Mott Foundation, the W. K. Kellogg Foundation, and the Nature Conservancy funded this land purchase. The forest conservation easements helped to link up 2.5 million acres of protected forest lands, including state and national forests.

Two other TNC preserves on the eastern boundary of the watershed include the Little Two Hearted Lakes Preserve established in 1999 (744 acres) and the Swamp Lakes Preserve established in 1992 (550 acres). Almost 90 percent of the watershed is now protected by state land, TNC land, the Working Forest Conservation easement, and other commercial forest reserves.

These land deals are beneficial for the watershed, but let's not forget this "Big U.P. Deal" was dwarfed by the Treaty of Washington. In that "*deal*," the Odawa and Ojibwe tribes ceded 10 million acres of land in northern lower Michigan and the U.P. to the U.S. Government. These tribes had done a wonderful job of protecting these natural resources for centuries. Hopefully the "Big U.P. Deal" will help protect this land into the future, mirroring the historic stewardship of the Indigenous people.

CHAPTER 9

FLORA AND FAUNA

Flora—Blueberries and White Pines

Our family loves blueberries. There are acres and acres of wild blueberries in the watershed. Scouting, picking, and eating blueberries are a big part of our summer activities. Every summer is different; the yield depends on the weather. Just the right amount of rain can produce a bountiful year—too little rain, and the berries look and taste like a hard raisin. A late spring frost can result in slim pickings. Every year the timing is different, and the location with the best blueberries moves around. During August, and sometimes July and September, we can have fresh blueberry pancakes every day. There was a time when our three young daughters were the perfect pickers: they were low to the ground, they enjoyed the picking, and they enjoyed the eating. Our former dog Jac was also a good picker. He did not share.

The 2008/2020 Two Hearted Watershed Management Plan describes the watershed flora and fauna, including threatened and endangered species. I have never heard of some of these plants, but it is nice to know that they exist, and that people care about them. These include English sundew, northern prostrate clubmoss, panicled screwstem, Wiegand's sedge, fir clubmoss, alga pondweed, black crowberry, and moor rush. These plants are all threatened or of special concern. They are part of a diverse mosaic of flora found in the fens, bogs, and marshes in the watershed as stated in the watershed plan:

> *The variety of wetland communities and the complexity of the peat-land forest ecosystem found within the Two Hearted River watershed are incomparable within the Great Lakes region. This landscape remains un-fragmented and relatively undeveloped. The high density of natural communities and broad expanse supports a great number of species including wide-ranging mammals such as black bear, fisher, pine marten and moose.*

In addition to the blueberries, the dunes in the jack pine forest between Boggy's and Lake Superior are covered in huckleberries, moss, and lichen. The boreal forest is normally where reindeer lichen is found. Here, the plant is found on the south-facing side of the dune slopes. The lichen is white and turns crispy under the summer sun. The green moss on the north-facing side of the hills stays soft all summer. These rolling hills are one of the few places one could take me blindfolded on a cloudy day, spin me around, and I could still tell you which direction is north, south, east, or west. The east-west ridges and the vegetation are consistent throughout this peninsula.

Boggy's Ten-footers

The trees we really appreciate are the ancient white pines along the river. When we bought Boggy's, we took note of six huge eastern white pine trees within 100 yards of our camp. The logging men who originally felled the virgin forests at the turn of the last century would have seen these trees, but they left them. The white pine is the state tree of Michigan.

The white pines still standing are in the river flood plain, and down a steep bank. This made access for the loggers difficult. We have estimates of their age at about 200 years. They all are (or were) over 10 feet in girth (circumference) at breast height (4.3 feet off the ground). Four of the trees were on a little rise in the middle of the oxbow just upstream of Boggy's, one tree is just across the river in the view from our cabin, and one is just downstream. Measuring tree diameters and girth at breast height is a standard, consistent way foresters measure trees, so that data can be compared.

The tall pines stick up above all other trees, and the sun brightens their branches early in the morning and late in the evening. The remaining forest is dark. The pines are located in low areas that are normally flooded in the spring. This annual flooding brings moisture; also sediment and nutrients settle out and help improve their habitat. We were told that before we bought the place, you could see these white pines over a mile from Boggy's as you walked back from the beach. The jack pines north of us have grown taller and block the view.

The painting on the cover was completed by artist and friend Kaye Krapohl. This painting was based on Plein Air paintings Kaye completed on a ski trip into Boggy's in March 2010. Kaye backpacked twice the amount of gear as the rest of us. Her bags filled with paints, brushes, and boards. The huge leaning white pine visible in the painting, glowing in the setting sun, broke off near its base in 2016.

I measured the girth of each tree in 2008 or 2010, and then again in 2022 for the survivors. They are listed as follows:

Location of eastern white pine measurements	Girth, 2008 or 2010	Girth, July 2022
Oxbow, NW	10 feet, 1 inch	Top blew off, 2018
Oxbow, NE	10 feet, 2 inches	10 feet, 11 inches
Oxbow, SW	10 feet, 9 inches	Died, 2013
Oxbow, SE	10 feet, 11 inches (Leaning over river, can be seen in Krapohl painting)	Broke off at base, 2016, created river bridge
Downstream	10 feet, 1 inch	10 feet, 7 inches
Across River	10 feet, 1 inch	10 feet, 10 inches

The table above is a way to track, and in a small way, honor the big pines. We care about these special beings, the history they have seen, the presence they have, how they pass on their gifts to their offspring. The Two Hearted River has many more of these that we enjoy from the canoe, standing guard over the river. Because of our interest in the big white pines, we found a state-wide database maintained by the Michigan Botanical Club. This database lists many large native and non-native trees located within the State of Michigan. On the February 2022 list, the top four white pines were all located in the U.P., with two of the four located within a few miles of Boggy's.

On July 2, we tracked one of these down, located next to the East Branch of the Two Hearted, just south of County Road 414. We obtained the coordinates off the MBC list and transferred that onto USGS quadrangle maps. We trekked through some sparse woods, then slid down a steep hill, and found a large white pine in the flood plain. We measured that one (girth of about 10 feet), and then saw the tree—she was unmistakable, located 100 feet away. This tree was at that time the largest scoring eastern white pine in Michigan, with a score of 333 points. We measured the girth at 14 feet, 8 inches. The height listed in the database was 143 feet. The score considers the girth, height, and spread of the crown. Within about 15 feet of this champion, all on the same little hummock raised slightly above the floor of the lowland, stood two more white pines with girths of over 11

Michigan Champion eastern white pine along East Branch of Two Hearted, July 2022.

feet. The mosquitos were horrible in this quiet little spot, out of the wind, on an early July morning. Laura suggested that later in the summer or in the fall might be a better time to track some of the other giants.

Woodlands and Wetlands

Boggy's two-acre property is a tree nursery. Hundreds of white pines, balsam fir, and white spruce seedlings and saplings cover the ground, along with maple, oak, and birch. Many of the large trees are jack pines. The jack pine surrounding our property in the state forest are about 40 years old. There are very few small trees, just moss, lichen, blueberries, ferns, and the jack pines.

The jack pine on our property are around 100 years old. They resemble palm trees with all their branches near the top, and slender trunks swaying in the wind. One can see our property line to the north, where our old pines meet the jack pine plantation. The old jack pines are dying and provide fuel for our sauna and campfires. The dying jack pines are being replaced with white pine, fir, and maple. These trees have all grown noticeably taller in our time at Boggy's. There is also one exceptionally large red pine in this area, and a few more small ones that we planted 20 years ago. There are also blueberry bushes and ferns in the understory throughout the property.

The forest along the river corridor is vastly different, a ribbon of green from forest floor to canopy. There are large white pine, jack pine, fir, spruce, oak, and maple trees, along with tag alder and red dogwood shrubs on the riverbank. The exception to this is the stretch of exposed sand bank on the river that continues to lose trees and shrubs—both those we've planted, and those that have been there a long time. There were two large red pines in this stretch at the toe of the bank. Fishing pressure caused erosion and exposed their roots. Eventually the river took the trees, their roots, and a portion of the bank away during the spring flood. In the summer, several varieties of wildflowers bloom along the river's edge.

Near our west property line, on top of the bank, our girls built a fort when they were small—a simple structure with scavenged logs and limbs. The fort was hidden from view of the cabin. The fort evolved to have welcome signs and seating, and a teeter-totter and swing nearby. I know the girls enjoyed this little refuge, where they could build what they wanted, away from the parents. It provided hours of entertainment and education about the woods, structures, and negotiating with siblings. The forest has reclaimed the fort, and it is waiting to be rebuilt by grandchildren.

Annie, Claire, and Julia in Boggy's fort, 2000.

The natural river program has a 100-foot setback from the river where no tree removal can take place. We have followed that ideal, even though we did not know about the policy until recently. We have planted many trees on our property: to diversify the jack pine, to reduce erosion along the river, and to close off the old two-track. We planted a white pine sapling about 20 years ago to block off the old two-track that lazy folks used to drive right to the top of the riverbank. Interestingly, we brought home a similar white pine and planted it in our side yard about the same time. Both trees look healthy, but the TC white pine is about twice as large as the one on the riverbank. The urban tree has been nurtured and watered, decorated with the occasional Christmas lights. The riverbank white pine has had to deal with drought, blizzard snow depths, and everything in between.

The beavers and the river do not know about the Natural River tree removal policy, and they have both removed trees on our property. Nature continues to do what it does, ever changing. Luckily, there is a thick vein of gravel at the level of the river. This gravel creates the gravel beds in the river that attract the fish and serves to armor the shore as the sand erodes away.

The forests, which define the watershed more than anything, have changed over the past 200 years. Initially the big white pines were cut and used for lumber for building ships, buildings, and structural support for mines. Some of the pines escaped the loggers, including the 200-year-old white pines near Boggy's, and the more than 400-year-old white pine we visited in the East Branch flood plain.

There are four million acres of state forests, and three million acres of national forests in Michigan. There is a total of 19 million total acres of forests in Michigan. There is a property tax exemption program to encourage private landowners to sustainably manage their forests for timber harvesting, but also wildlife habitat and other resource improvement.

The commercial forest act was intended to help landowners retain and manage the millions of privately held acres of Michigan forests. The program provides tax incentives to manage forests, while allowing foot access to the public for hiking, hunting, and fishing. In the Two Hearted watershed, thousands of acres are in the commercial forest program and are managed under the supervision of professional foresters. Boggy's property is only two acres, so we do not even qualify for the commercial forest program which has a 40-acre minimum.

The watershed has 56,000 acres of wetlands, 21,000 acres of which are non-forested wetlands. These wetlands have not been impacted by man. There is peat in the wetlands, and peat is excellent at storing carbon. Worldwide, about three percent of all land is peat. That small percentage of peat stores 30% of the land-based carbon. Peat is the planet's most efficient carbon sink. Peat thrives in wetlands that have high precipitation and low temperatures. A quote from a September 2022 article by Keith Matheny in the *Detroit Free Press* stated, "*A square meter of U.P. or Canadian peatland holds five times the carbon as a square meter of Amazon rainforest.*" Threats to the peat in the Two Hearted watershed include drying out and burning. It takes 1,000 years to form one meter of peat, but this peat can be destroyed quickly.

The abundant natural resources of the Two Hearted River watershed have been well described. Natural capital accounting provides a value for our natural assets. Natural capital is the unimpaired environmental assets (e.g., air, water, land, flora, fauna, etc.) in a region. There are three major components: 1) nonrenewable resources (oil, minerals), 2) renewable resources (fish, wood, drinking water), and 3) environmental services (maintain air quality, water quality, the hydrologic cycle and climate, recycling of nutrients, soil health, and pollination). Currently our nation's Gross National Product (GDP) does not recognize these assets.

Our family spent four months in 1993 in Mérida, Venezuela. I was volunteering for CIDIAT, an environmental research organization that was part of the Universidad de los Andes (ULA). We met and became friends with a Venezuelan scientist, Sara Aniyar. Sara was affiliated with ULA and was studying the economic value of healthy coral reefs. Reefs around the world were being impacted by warming waters due to climate change. In addition, polluted stormwater runoff impacts near-shore reefs. The concept of putting a price tag on intact natural resources was new to me. She eventually came to conduct additional research in the College of Agricultural and Natural Resources at Michigan State University and we reconnected.

MSU and other land grant institutions have been actively researching how to quantify natural capital. In the Two Hearted watershed, the woodlands and wetlands provide water and air quality benefits. The benefits to the water include regulating and slowing the flow of water, filtering out pollution, and shading the stream to lower water temperature. Carbon sequestration is also an increasingly important value of these natural resources. In an unpopulated watershed like the Two Hearted, the amount of carbon sequestered by the natural environment is much greater than the carbon dioxide released by human endeavors.

Decades of research are now being put into practice. There are efforts at the federal level to include these natural assets in the national system of economic accounting. It is surprising to me that this concept was studied at the university level 30 years ago, and only now is being acted upon. The annual change in natural asset wealth would be included with the GDP. A tree in a forest has value if it is not cut down, like our ancient white pines. I applaud efforts to account for that.

The Two Hearted River watershed is overflowing with natural assets. Do we even know the value of a mature forest, a functional wetland, or a clear flowing stream? Recent books such as *The Treeline: The Last Forest and the Future of Life on Earth*; and *Finding the Mother Tree: Discovering the Wisdom of the Forest*, explain how much we have learned, but also how little we still know about forests, how trees communicate, and the full value of this resource.

One overlooked part of the forest, hidden underground, is the fungi. Over 90% of plant species rely on fungi to survive, and more is being learned about their role. Hidden just below the forest floor lie mycorrhizal fungi that make up one third to one half of the living mass of soil. Society is realizing the importance of this fungi, especially considering the role it plays in climate change.

Fauna—the Animals We Share the Watershed With

In October 2010 I had just retired, and we were empty nesters with Julia off to MSU. We decided to mark these two significant life events by spending the entire month of October at the camp. Each morning we walked down the road to the "plumber's bend," a fast-moving stretch of river about a half-mile upstream of Boggy's. Every visit, like clockwork, there was a blue heron standing there fishing. Laura wrote in her journal from a bird's eye view:

Who are these invaders? I fish and dine in the privacy of my bend. The big sweeping bend with a long, shallow, sparkling gravel bed. There is the remnants of an aged mighty white pine that leaned for many years across the bend. It leaned and split and moaned and groaned and finally gave way, and was eventually carried downstream with a wall of force with the spring breakup of the river. The stump remains, sprouted with new growth.

So, who are these intruders? I know what the fishermen want. I share the bounty of the river with them. They try to mimic me, standing in the chilly waters, occasionally catching a fish. They are thrilled with their success, but it wouldn't be enough to sustain life. Perhaps the fishermen should try to use a long spear as I do?

The intruders do not come to fish. They stand on two legs and have a wolf-like partner on four. They just stand and look. We exchange stares and I am leery of them. They have come many mornings to disturb my hunt. Sometimes I spread my wide wings and move on to a less favorable bend. Sometimes I hide and wait for the intruders to leave.

I will be leaving soon as the days get shorter and colder. I will seek another

*quiet bend, somewhere warmer, and leave this bend to the fishermen and those
that watch from the bluff.*

Spending more time allows for further reflection. We bought a pumpkin
and carved a calendar grid on the face. Every day we carved a symbol that
represented something special about the day; a full moon, animal sightings,
Spartan football victory over University of Michigan (we listened on the
radio), a bike ride to Grand Marais, visits by friends, big waves at the big
lake, pancakes, etc. This pumpkin was our calendar, so we could keep track
of what day it was.

We did not have a cell phone (or cell service if we had), so we would
cycle to Deer Park each Sunday to catch up with our three girls and Laura's
mom on the pay phone. They would call us at 15-minute intervals.

Animals we listed in the Boggy's Camp journal that month included
bald eagles, two river otters, pygmy shrew, snow bunting, snowy owl, barred
owl, and the blue heron. We also heard coyotes howl, saw moose tracks on
the CCI road, and bear tracks on a two-track east of Holland Lake State
Forest Campground.

*Our month stay at Boggy's was fantastic. We found that it is a fleeting moment
in time and calls to us to come back another time, perhaps for a longer stay. We
had no big agendas, just to enjoy our time here and together, and we did both
with complete success. We took the gift of time, and simply lived.*
Boggy's Camp Journal, Laura, October 29, 2010

In addition to the many listed threatened and endangered species in the watershed, many others have been part of our Boggy's experience. When you
spend time at a place out of doors, in different seasons and weather conditions, and without TV or internet, we notice things.

*Springtime at Boggy's . . . the maple leaves are just beginning to come out
and are a striking shade of red. The ferns are up, with leaves held tightly at
the ends, unfurrowed like they are trying to stay warm. We were visited each
morning by the call of a common flicker. The woodpecker has made a hole
(nest) at the top of the standing dead white pine that overlooks the bend of the
river. When the sun edges its way to the bird's home, they greet the day in song.*

It has been interesting to see that happen each morning. I wonder about the multitude of things happening regularly like that I take no notice of and miss.
Boggy's Camp Journal, Laura, May 18–23, 2022

We have seen some rare animals through the years, and some that are just fun to see. My most unusual and memorable encounter happened when I was cycling up the High Banks Trail and encountered a fisher on a very windy day. The fisher came out of the woods, walked right in front of me, and then quickly turned around. I jumped off my bike and tried to see it travelling down the bank towards the river, but it was gone, out of sight. A fisher is a shy omnivore that inhabits mature forests and is the largest member of the weasel family with long dark fur.

We notice many different plants and animals, a few of them make a bigger impression, and always get a mention in Boggy's journal reports:

Black Bears—We see a bear mounted on the cabin wall every time we visit. We don't know the story, but the bear looks old, his nose is degraded and needs a little black paint. I have seen just one live black bear since we have had the cabin. I was mountain biking, a quiet way to sneak around in the woods. The bear crossed a county road, just ahead of me. We have seen bear prints many times, and a lot of scat. In the summer when the blueberries are out in force, the bears are also. Huge scat piles of what looks like lightly digested blueberries are seen in the woods near our cabin.

Paul Campbell, a longtime camp host at the Two Hearted River State Forest Campground at the river mouth, told me he had a too-close run-in with bears. He was picking blueberries north of our camp near Lake Superior with his two sons in the 1980s. They noticed a bear cub crying up in a tree near them. Paul spotted the mother bear coming towards them. Paul and his kids made noise and backed away towards the big lake. The mother bear followed them towards the lake. Paul thought they might need to take a swim to escape. Eventually, the bears disappeared into the woods.

Todd, a member of the East Branch Sportsmen's Club told us another bear story. He had been coming to the EBSC since boyhood. When Todd was young, they used to feed bears outside their cabin. They would put up some pans so that when the bears came during the night, they would hear them. His family would get up and watch them with flashlights. Not surprisingly, the bears became acclimated to the folks in the cabin and started coming during the day. His parents quit feeding the bears.

Hunting for black bears is common in the early fall. Dogs are used to track and tree bears. We often see pickup trucks with multiple dogs in little wood boxes. We see the hunters traversing the forest roads or camping at the nearby Reed and Green SFCG. We have also heard the dogs on chase. One time we heard dogs howling when we were at Boggy's. We heard them south across the river, getting closer and closer. I was watching from the bank, expecting the bear at any time to come out of the woods and swim across the river. The bear eluded the dogs and us.

Coyote—We hear yips and howls at night and see their tracks but have only had one good look at a coyote. We were out snowshoeing during blizzard-like conditions, and a coyote came quickly over a little rise. We stared at each other, eye to eye. The coyote turned and went back from whence they came, but it was an exciting close-up view. The wind muffled our sounds and diluted our smell.

Moose—We have not seen a moose but have seen scat and tracks when we have visited McMahon Lake Preserve. Kristie Sitar, MDNR wildlife biologist, reports that these moose are not part of the helicopter lift that placed Canadian moose in the U.P. west of Marquette in the mid-1980s. They are part of either the original moose herd native to the U.P. or have immigrated on their own from Canada. There are about 100 moose in the eastern U.P., and about 400 in the area west of Marquette.

Wolves—We also have not seen a wolf but have heard reports from neighbors and campers who have seen them. There are about 700 wolves in the U.P., 100 of them in the eastern U.P. I reviewed a recent report by Kristie Sitar and Brian Roell with the MDNR titled "Factors Limiting Deer Abundance in the Upper Peninsula." Interesting conclusions from the report are that the severity of the winter is more important than wolf predation in determining deer numbers. There were few severe winters in 1980–1995. A severe winter is defined as 90 days of a foot or more of snow. Since that time, there have been numerous severe winters, and deer numbers have dropped accordingly. Other interesting findings in the study are that wolves are the fourth most deadly predator for fawns. Coyotes, black bear, and bobcats all take more fawns than wolves. Also, when wolves do take a deer, it will most often be in March or April, when the deer is already weak and may die of starvation.

Whitetail Deer—Most of the old camps were built to hunt deer, and just as importantly, to host *"deer camp."* Big whitetail bucks used to frequent the area. Boggy's Camp has two eleven-point deer mounts on the wall. The one tag is dated 1944. The two deer have locked antlers. The story passed down to us was that when the hunter came upon the bucks, one was already dead when the other was shot.

11-point deer mounts, Boggy's Camp.

We do not see many deer, maybe because we normally have a dog with us. Deer tracks are plentiful on all our hikes. One recent early December morning there was snow on the ground, but not enough to ski. We were walking on the North Country Trail north of our camp and saw an area of blood-stained snow just off the trail. There were canine tracks everywhere, and just a few remaining bones and deer fur. There was not much of the deer left, and the bones were clean. Some ravens were hanging around. The tracks were the size of a coyote, not wolves. Our dog Marta was incredibly nervous, probably because of strong coyote scent.

Beavers—Beavers made an immediate impression on us after we bought Boggy's Camp. The former owner had planted a dozen conifers on the riverbank to stabilize the sand. We arrived one weekend to find them gone. I had thought beavers only chewed down birch and poplar. All the small trees were gone, just a few wood chips remaining. The beavers also chewed halfway through a small paper birch we had growing next to the cabin. I protected the birch with a section of stove pipe in case the beaver returned. After about 10 years, I removed the stove pipe, and the tree has now grown into a 25-foot-tall mature tree.

Trappers almost wiped out North American beavers in the 17th, 18th, and 19th centuries to supply a European obsession for beaver hats. The U.P. wilderness was left mostly untouched by colonists because it was rugged and remote. With the mid-18th century discovery of iron ore, things changed, and the U.P. population grew. When Henry Lewis Morgan visited Marquette in the U.P. in 1855 to study beavers, they were plentiful. Morgan was an attorney and anthropologist from New York hoping to tap into U.P. iron ore fortunes. At that time, creeks had strings of beaver ponds all along them. The hydrology of these watersheds had been changed by thousands of years of beaver families. The Two Hearted watershed had also been impacted by generations of beavers, especially in the wetlands of the upper reaches of the watershed.

Since the early 1900s, there has been a widespread practice in the United States removing beaver dams and trapping beavers to protect trout and roads. Road commissions remove the dams affecting their roads, and angler organizations also remove dams and trap beavers. There had been long-held beliefs that the dams warm the stream temperature which negatively affects cold-water-loving trout. Researchers in the past 20 years have pushed back on these myths. Scott McGill, a founder of an environmental restoration company, is quoted in Leila Philip's book *Beaverland*:

Fishery folks at the state level have this idea that if it is a beaver pond it has to increase water temperature and so beaver and trout can't coexist. But they coevolved over millions of years, so that is very absurd if you think about it.

McGill found no difference in water temperature upstream and down-stream of a beaver dam in upstate New York. In addition, the deeper water in beaver dams allow trout to swim deeper to avoid blue heron, a common predator of young trout.

Mountain Lions (Cougars)—Once, when canoeing to the mouth, I saw a flash of a light brown animal that disappeared in the woods. The animal's hind end did not look like a deer. I still kick myself for not stopping the canoe and getting out to look for tracks. There have been many confirmed sightings of cougars in the U.P. These appear to all be young males that range widely. Biologist Sitar indicated the MDNR have no evidence of female cougars, or young, in the eastern U.P.

Kirtland's Warbler—This is one of the rarest songbirds in North America. The Kirtland only breeds in young jack pines in Michigan and adjacent parts of Wisconsin and Ontario. In the burn area from the Duck Lake Fire 25 singing males were detected in 2022. Fires give and take away.

Spruce Grouse—This rare native grouse has been protected in Michigan since 1915. Many "birders" have this bird unfulfilled on their life list. The spruce grouse is common in the woods around and north of Boggy's. We often have a family of them walk along the riverbank, and they seem to not mind us being there. We also often see them in the jack pine along the forest road headed towards Lake Superior. If a dog is with us, they simply fly up into the nearest tree and wait for us to pass.

Bob and I (and Jac) didn't make it back here for the two weeks we had hoped for at this busy time when kids needed to be at various places. But we were able to carve out one glorious peaceful week that I am thankful for . . .

Some highlights of the week included a few hikes to the Big Lake, one with a dip and an eagle viewing, the other at sunset with a bottle of wine. We had a brood of spruce grouse chicks (4) and mom hanging around camp eating ants.

When I went out to take a photo, one bold chick pecked an ant off my sandal and ate it. I got a great close-up shot . . .

Today we paddled to the mouth. The river is down considerably, and it was a slow trip. Big winds blew dark and white clouds in and out when we were mostly looking for the warmth of the sun. The Big Lake was rolling when we arrived at the mouth with at least 8-foot waves. The most exciting part of the trip were the two young bald eagles we came upon on an island in the river. They took off, and one circled around, while the other sat in a nearby tree for great viewing.

Boggy's Camp Journal, Laura, August 17, 2007

Here is a newspaper clipping from the September 9, 1934, *Escanaba Daily Press.* The "partridge" Boggy saw was a ruffed or spruce grouse. I am sure the logging of the previous 50 years had an impact on their populations. It appears from the article they may have disappeared for a while but were making a comeback.

So Boggy was hanging around the original Reed and Green Bridge in the early 1930s. This is only about 500 feet from the location of Boggy's Camp. Had he built the cabin by then, or was he just enjoying the area? Maybe he had a canvas tent encampment, getting ready for hunting season? This is the earliest mention I have found of Boggy Young near Boggy's Camp.

PARTRIDGE APPEAR TO BE PLENTIFUL

Are the partridge coming back to these parts? Conservation men say they do not think so. But several citizens have seen fair sized flocks during the past few weeks. Boggy Young saw a hen and a half dozen chicks at the Reed and Green Bridge over the Little Two Heart the other day. The birds were so tame they stood still on the sandy background and let Boggy take their picture.

Escanaba Daily Press, September 9, 1934

CHAPTER 10

FIRE

Our family has always enjoyed Boggy's proximity to Lake Superior. We hike there all year around, just to see the big lake and walk along the deserted beach. We often bring back too many heavy stones because there are just so many beautiful ones. We sometimes have a campfire and swim in the short window of tolerable water temperature that occurs in late summer. The U.P. is known for biting insects; bumper stickers show the mosquito as the U.P. state bird. However, the stable flies on the Lake Superior beach are to me the most annoying. They congregate with a south wind and attack exposed skin. You can't swat them like mosquitos—they are too fast. A north wind dissipates them.

We were sitting on the Lake Superior beach at a remote dead end of a forest road, just west of Boggy's. We were getting ready to cook some hot dogs. We had a small fire going, waiting for coals to appear. It was a cool late summer day, with the wind out of the north. Suddenly, a woman came running out from a nearby camp, yelling at us about the fire. She said there was a recent small fire near their camp, and, living in the woods, they were always conscious of the potential danger. Our fire was in the sand, and we were trying to be careful. We lacked awareness of how others might view our behavior. We were surprised there was even anyone around.

A small percentage of Michigan wildfires are caused by lightning strikes. Most fires are caused by human activity and carelessness. Forest fires pose advantages and disadvantages to a watershed. They are a naturally occurring event, and our forests and wetland plants and animals have evolved to survive them. Our modern suppression of fires has created a different type of forest that burns hotter than in the past. Advantages of wildfires include the stimulation of new green shoots, opening of impenetrable growth, restoration of nutrients to the soil, and the release of seeds in some species. Jack pine are an example of trees that need heat to open their cones. Kirtland warblers are rare birds that need young jack pine forests to nest in. They have evolved with fires clearing out the old jack pine trees, spurring new growth.

Historically, the Ojibwe used fire to maintain healthy populations of red pines and wild blueberries. The thick bark of the red pines is fire resistant, and their resin was used by the tribes for waterproofing birch bark canoes. The open canopy under the red pines was, and still is, a wonderful place for wild blueberries to grow. Small fires would reduce the fuel and inhibit large wildfires by burning overgrown vegetation, as well as stimulate growth for blueberries. Harvesting and storing blueberries for winter food, and utilizing canoes for transport, were life and death issues for Ojibwe culture.

Research conducted in the Boundary Water Canoe Area in northern Minnesota has used tree ring data from old red pines to determine the frequency of fire. Data has shown that before about 1900, regular fires were set by the Indigenous people. After 1900, government policies banned all fires. One result in this change in policy is that some of the desirable qualities that created the BWCA—the many islands with open areas dominated by large red pine and blueberries—became overgrown with other species. These areas were used for camping during canoe travel by the Indigenous people, and then by the early visitors to the BWCA. The lack of fires in this wilderness area made it less desirable.

Disadvantages of fires include, of course, potential loss of human life and structures, loss of animals and habitat, along with an increase in stream water temperature due to a loss of shade. There can also be a loss of filtering of surface water due to a loss of vegetation, and the burning of peat soils.

Sleeper Lake Fire

*We were a little cautious about coming up here because of all of the reports on
the Sleeper Lake Forest Fire and were waiting for the predicted wind shift to
the north. The fire was the largest the UP has seen in 25 years, over 18,500
acres burned. There were road closings, assistance brought in from Minnesota,
Ontario and the National Guard and Governor Granholm declared it a dis-
aster area. We were surprised when driving up that we saw very little evidence
other than numerous emergency vehicles stationed along County Road 407.*

Boggy's Camp Journal, Laura, August 17, 2007

On August 2, 2007, a lightning strike started a wildfire near Sleeper Lake.
Sleeper Lake is in the Two Hearted watershed, about six miles north of
Newberry, and east of County Road 407. The fire initially blew to the
south with a north wind, then the wind shifted to the southeast and the fire
moved north. High winds fueled the fire. Firefighters contained the fire by
the end of September 2007. Over 18,000 acres were burned, including over
1,000 acres of commercial forest land, according to the Two Hearted River
Watershed Plan. This fire was the third largest fire in modern Michigan history. There were larger fires in the late 1800s after logging removed many
of the larger trees and left their branches for fuel. The Sleeper Lake Fire re-
sulted in no loss of life, and only one structure was lost.

Assessments of the burned area in September 2007 indicated no impact
to the fish community. In the spring of 2008, the watershed had greened
up. During the spring of 2008, less than one year after the fire, the marsh-
land of the Two Hearted watershed and other areas impacted by the Sleeper
Lake fire were reported to be substantially re-vegetated and the fire boundary was no longer visible.

The fire was fought by 240 people. Three State Forest Campgrounds
(SFCG) were closed. In addition, Muskallonge State Park was closed for a
period, negatively impacting the only store in the area, Deer Park Lodge, at
the height of the tourist season.

Duck Lake Fire

A second major fire in the watershed began on May 24, 2012. This fire was
also started by a lightning strike and replaced the Sleeper Lake Fire as the

state's third largest fire, with over 21,000 acres burned. The fire was contained by the middle of June 2012.

Laura and I were travelling in southern Ontario when friends contacted us to see if we had heard of the U.P. fire, and whether Boggy's Camp was OK. What fire? We had heard nothing. We quickly looked up the news to find the extent of the fire, and the direction of its advance. Not that we could do anything about it.

The fire started near Duck Lake, which is part of the Little Two Hearted Lakes just north of M-123. The fire was blown north by a strong south wind and marched about 13 miles to the shore of Lake Superior. The wind then shifted to the west and blew the fire easterly. When the fire was out, the western edge of the burn was about three miles east of Boggy's Camp. Others were not so lucky. The fire burned 136 structures, including 49 cabins and homes. Rainbow Lodge, a motel, cabins, and a store with a canoe livery near the mouth of the Two Hearted was shut down because of the fire. The popular Two Hearted SFCG was closed for a period, along with Culhane Lake and Pike Lake SFCG. The fire also caused the closure of Tahquamenon Falls State Park for the Memorial Day holiday.

Richard Robinson, owner of Rainbow Lodge, remembers the fire: *"A very windy day, the fire burned 12 miles north in 7 hours, then the wind turned, and it blew east and burned 5 miles in 3 hours."* He and his wife, Kathy, left Rainbow Lodge to stay with friends on Little Lake, about three miles to the northeast. Amazingly, two cabins on their property were untouched, along with the gas pumps. Water dropped by rescue helicopters saved the gas pumps. Most of the resort buildings were lost.

Mike Brown, the owner of Deer Park Lodge, remarked that even from County Road 407, it looked like most of the forest east of them was on fire, due to the bright orange glow and smoke odor. He was surprised that the fire was 10 miles to the east.

The fire was fought by 300 people. They built 43 miles of fire break, many by hand. The *Newberry News* noted that Newberry and Luce County residents lined the roads and cheered on workers as they left for the evening.

CHAPTER 11

STATE AND NATIONAL RECOGNITION

The Two Hearted River and watershed has received state and national recognition over the past few decades. The Two Hearted is distinguished as a Michigan Natural River, the only one to receive a Wilderness Designation.

The Two Hearted River Natural River Plan

The Michigan Department of Natural Resources published the Two Hearted River Natural River Plan in 1973. The plan provides a description of the river and watershed and a plan for protection. The Michigan Department of Natural Resources developed the plan in cooperation with the Luce County Planning Commission and Zoning Board. To help inform the plan, the Fisheries Division of the MDNR prepared a plan titled *Two Hearted River: Leland Anderson,* dated October 1973.

The Natural River Plan had support from many, but not everyone. A Two Hearted River property owner who had attended public hearings on the plan made his displeasure known in a letter to the editor of the *Sault Ste. Marie News.*

Be it hereby known that I am in favor of the spirit and concept of Wild River Act in its relationship to our Two Hearted River, but I am opposed with all of the vim and vigor at my command to the infringements on the time-honored rights of the individual property owner.

In my opinion, it smirks of the teachings of Marx, Lenin and Mao—take everything from one class of society and give it to another . . .

If this act is adopted in its proposed form then we on the Two Hearted are through, washed up, get out.

After another public hearing, the DNR changed the plan: 1) reducing the width of the protected strip on each side of the river from one-quarter mile (1,320 feet) to 400 feet; 2) assuring that the protection would be administered by local government entities; and 3) expanding the protection to include the mainstream and the tributaries. The Michigan Natural Resources Commission then approved the Two Hearted River Natural River plan. The commission granted 70 miles of the river's mainstream and tributaries special protection as the state's first "Wilderness River."

The Natural River program in Michigan currently includes 16 rivers, with two in the U.P. (the Fox River and the Two Hearted). The zoning rules for all the rivers have been updated by the state and the new rules were effective September 19, 2013. The rules provide for a zoning district 400 feet wide on both sides of the river. New buildings within that zone have a 100-foot setback from the river, and most new commercial development is prohibited. Existing structures like Boggy's Camp, built before 1973, are grandfathered and do not need to be moved or removed. A natural vegetative strip does need to be maintained within 100 feet of the river. Luce County administers the zoning restrictions on private property. "The Wilderness Designation" does not contain any special conditions but is taken into consideration when the MDNR fishery, forestry, wildlife, and parks and recreation divisions make decisions in the watershed.

The Two Hearted Wild River National Park

Additional protections were sought for the Two Hearted watershed in the 1980s. The National Park Service identified the watershed as one of the few nationally that remained undeveloped. The NPS proposed creating a national wilderness river park to preserve the 125,000 acres of land along the Two Hearted for future generations. The Blackwater River in Maryland and the Amicalola River in Georgia were also considered. The Park Service already had a Wild and Scenic Rivers program that protected stretches of rivers. The idea of the national wilderness park was to preserve the entire watershed.

In July of 1988, William Penn Mott, the Director of the National Park Service, flew over Pictured Rocks, Sleeping Bear Dunes, and Isle Royale National Park. One reason for the flight was to consider the addition of Grand Island to Pictured Rocks National Lakeshore, and to look at the Two Hearted watershed. Cleveland-Cliffs had put Grand Island up for sale in the 1980s. The primary purpose of the flight was to provide Mott an aerial view of the Two Hearted watershed so he could advance the concept of a National River Park. Pictured Rocks superintendent Grant Petersen, who was on the flight that day, said Mott showed little interest in promoting Grand Island as an addition to the National Lakeshore. Mott was interested in the Two Hearted.

Congressman Robert Davis was not supportive. He represented Michigan's 11th Congressional District, which at that time included all the U.P., and a portion of the northern lower peninsula. Davis, who was born and raised in the U.P., also served in the Michigan house and senate from 1966 to 1978. The March 16, 1988, *Newberry News* quoted a Davis news release:

> *"The Upper Peninsula forest products industry is doing extremely well. Prospects are encouraging for future expansion of the industry in Luce County. This expansion would be threatened, however, by Park Service acquisition of the property along the Two Hearted River and its tributaries." The article further stated that approximately 40 percent of the land area of the 11th District already is state or federally owned. Pointing to what he called "excessive government encroachment on private land," Davis said any further government acquisitions would be harmful to the forest products industry and the economy of Northern Michigan.*

Davis won, and the National Park Service backed off on its plans. Battle lines were drawn; preserve nature and the elusive "wilderness" amenities people crave or use natural resources to provide jobs.

In April 1989, Mott, who was the director of the National Park Service from 1985 to 1989, told the *San Francisco Examiner* he had two chief regrets about his time at the service: failing to persuade Congress to authorize two new national parks: the Tallgrass Prairie National Park, and the Big Two Hearted Wild River National Park. Director Mott had graduated with a degree in landscape architecture from Michigan State University in 1931. He must have had an affinity for Michigan. One of his regrets was resolved when the 10,894-acre Tallgrass Prairie National Preserve in Kansas was created as the 370th national park unit on November 12, 1996.

When I found out the potential Two Hearted Wild River National Park was shot down, my first reaction was that it was a loss for the U.P. and for Michigan. This planned recognition also confirmed my belief that the Two Hearted is unique. But on further reflection, maybe Congressman Davis was right. Lately, many National Parks are under tremendous pressure from tourists wanting to visit. For me, the beauty of any park is diminished when every nook and cranny are filled with people and their cars. The Two Hearted River watershed has changed little since we bought Boggy's 30 years ago. Logging has been the most obvious change in the landscape, but we have been visiting long enough that even the clear-cuts have grown and recovered.

The negative impact of off-road vehicles has increased on the small forest roads. Some of the formerly green, mossy two-tracks have become rutted sandy roads, with no access for anything other than a high clearance, four-wheel drive vehicle. If the area was part of a national park, the impact from motorized vehicles on back roads would have been restricted and reduced, but total visitors to the watershed would have been much greater. Boggy's Camp would not have been for sale in 1991 if the property was in the middle of a national park.

Maintaining that precarious balance of resource protection versus exploitation is never-ending. These battles have gone on, and will go on, all over the world. Drafting this book has gotten us out to some remote locations within the Two Hearted watershed. In some of these places, we have felt we are truly in an isolated, wild, and beautiful place. The wilderness feels intact for now.

ACCESS AND DEVELOPMENT

CHAPTER 12

ROADS AND MOTORIZED ACCESS

For thousands of years, Indigenous people had seasonal camps at the river mouth and would have journeyed up the river by walking or via canoe for fishing, hunting, and food gathering. Otherwise, access to the watershed was limited.

In the 1600s and 1700s, the Jesuits were plying Lake Superior in canoes. The Jesuits learned the Ojibwe language and exploited their food sources. The Jesuit access into the interior of the watershed would have mirrored the Ojibwe.

In the 1840s and 1850s, State of Michigan surveyors walked every square mile of the watershed to lay out townships and sections. They left behind no structures but gained knowledge of the river and the huge white pines.

Interior access to the watershed opened as needed to reach the white pines. Logging of the pines first took place close to the Lake Superior shore, and then up the Two Hearted River. Horses dragged sleds full of logs to the river in the winter on iced-over haul roads. The logs would then be floated down the river in the spring.

The logger Culhane was the first to build rail lines to retrieve logs. He built his own temporary railroad lines to reach some of the trees distant from water. All of these old rail lines are gone, but we know of one significant unnatural cut into the riverbank west of High Banks Trail. The cut was made to flatten out the grade for a railroad to move logs from the high bank to the river.

The *Newberry News* has reports on some first roads and bridges built in the early years. A new road was constructed in 1888 from Newberry to Lake Superior at Deer Park. A new bridge was installed in 1895 over the Two Hearted along this road.

A 1915 map prepared by Cleveland-Cliffs showed a road roughly where County Road 407 is, and a road where County Road 414 is now. A road on what is now the alignment of our access road to Boggy's (County Road 410) was labelled as a "wagon road." This road continued easterly to connect to the Coast Guard Road, which then continued to the mouth of the Two Hearted River. At that time, the wagon road did not cross the river at the Reed and Green Bridge location near Boggy's. The old map also showed that Deer Park was connected to the Two Hearted River Life Saving Station at the mouth of the river (this sandy historic trail is now called the Coast Guard Road).

The original Reed and Green Bridge was built around 1915. The bridge provided access to the river, and folks started camping next to the road. The current Reed and Green State Forest Campground is located where this original bridge was. This bridge was removed and rebuilt about one mile upstream in the 1980s. This change removed the steep hill on the south side of the river. I have heard several firsthand stories of the difficulty in climbing that rutted, gravel hill, immediately after crossing the narrow bridge. This steep gravel road would have also dumped tons of sediment into the river during rainstorms.

Vehicles have changed with the times. In the early part of the 20th century, roads were not particularly good, often gravel, or washboard through swamps, and filled with ruts or mud. The original motor cars were built with high ground clearance, and they could travel these old roads. People were also prepared to fix their cars. Here is a historical account of access to the watershed back in the 1920s, and adventures along the way.

Sleigh transportation between Newberry and Deer Park, around 1900.
Source: Deer Park Lodge

Agnes Potter Diary

I contacted Bill Knapp, president of the East Branch Sportsmen's Club, and
he gave me some history of the club, and the nearby Spile Dam Club. He
included an interesting diary of a woman married to one of the founders
of the Spile Dam Club, and the sister-in-law of the founder of the EBSC.
The diary described their early trips to the East Branch of the Two Hearted
River between 1925 and 1947. The entry below is their first trip travelling
to the U.P. from Flint, Michigan, for the 1925 deer hunting season.

> *November 1925—Harry and R.J. Potter, Everett, Agnes and Wava Potter,*
> *Edmond, Della & Kenneth Olson, Floyd Harkness, Art Harkness (brothers)*
> *went to Luce County Hunting.*
>
> *Friday, or Saturday, a.m. November 13—They left about midnight. Harry*
> *& R.J. had a new 1926 Oldsmobile—Della, Agnes & Wava rode with*
> *them—Everett had the Reo Roadster (old Rolls Ruff.) Edmond and Kenneth*
> *rode with him—Floyd and Art had an old Oldsmobile Touring Car (Perfor-*
> *mance Plus). Got to Houghton Lake about daylight. Something went wrong*
> *with the distributor in old Rolls Ruff. Harry put a shingle nail in it and they*

went on. At Levering the tongue broke in Floyd's trailer. Had to flip that back over, it was 3 pm when they got in line at Mackinaw City. It was quite a long wait—it was dark when they got to St. Ignace.

At St. Ignace they were in a store buying some groceries, mentioned they wished there was a vacant house they could sleep in. Two young men overheard them and told them if they wanted to drive 15 miles they could sleep in their barn—they had lots of straw they could put on the barn floor. They made a field bed of straw. Everyone just slept in their clothes.

Sun. Nov. 15th—ate breakfast at Miller's Camp. We all sat at a large table with a big bowl of cookies in the center while they were waiting for the food. They started eating cookies. When they brought their breakfast, they also re-filled the bowl of cookies. The roads were terrible. The first 8 miles north of Newberry was corduroy roads, with about every other log was gone.

They had a lot of trouble getting into the campsite. Every time the old Rolls Ruff scraped bottom—they knew they had to help the new Oldsmobile because it was lower and performance was even worse because they were hauling a large trailer loaded. Finally at midnight they arrived where they were going to camp. It took 3 hours to put up Floyd's 18'× 18' army tent. They got some-thing to eat, then laid down until daylight.

Agnes quote "I didn't want to come so I didn't enjoy the trip nor sitting in the car waiting for them to put up the tent. I said anyone that would come here once was a fool, and anyone that would come here twice was bigger fool. But after I had been here a few days I enjoyed being there."

Everett said "I had to fight with her to get her to come the first time, then I would have to fight with her to leave her home." (joking) but he always had her to go with him, wherever he went.

Monday, Nov. 16—the men worked all day putting up the rest of the tents.

The movement to build better, smoother roads across the state in the 1920s allowed people like the Potters to access the north country. A few dec-ades earlier, there were few paved roads or automobiles. The Potters found rough roads north of Newberry, but clear sailing from Flint to Newberry. Except, of course, the wait for the car ferry across the Straits of Mackinac. The Mackinac Bridge was not opened until 1957. The good roads allowed the state to promote the burned-over sand plains of the northern Lower Peninsula and the U.P. to southern Michiganders for fishing and hunting.

The majestic trees had been cut, but remote trout streams, tree-lined inland lakes, second generation forests, and the Great Lakes shorelines were an attraction. Many people I meet in Traverse City started coming to the area because of their family's historic connection to Northern Michigan's plentiful natural resources. Private automobiles transported these travelers "Up North" on the growing state highway network.

In the 1940s and '50s, the roads continued to improve, and regular family cars became larger, more comfortable, but lower to the ground. These vehicles became less useful to access remote lands via two-tracks and logging roads. Four-wheel drive Jeeps became popular after WWII and allowed sportsmen to more easily travel into the wilderness to reach cabins or fishing and hunting spots.

In the 1980s and '90s, sport utility vehicles (SUVs) became popular with the Ford Explorer, Chevy Blazer, and others. These vehicles combined high ground clearance, four-wheel drive, and yet the comfort of a passenger vehicle to get to the woods and trails.

At about the same time, the all-terrain vehicle (ATV) became popular. These were originally three-wheeled vehicles with motorcycle type controls and seats one would straddle. The three-wheeled ATVs were tippy and dangerous, and manufacturers quickly started selling four-wheeled versions. These vehicles were used by some to access cabins and fishing holes, but often were used just for recreation. Four-wheeling was an activity with growing popularity. The latest iteration is the side-by-side, which was developed for more comfort, and more passengers. An SxS has lots of power, room for up to four passengers, and some are enclosed and heated. They contain a roll cage for safety and high ground clearance to go anywhere.

Laura and I were driving down the CCI trail, west of Pine Stump in May of 2022. It was a cool Saturday morning, and we were planning to investigate some of the Nature Conservancy forest reserve lands. The road was a little rough, but firm enough for our low ground clearance two-wheel drive vehicle. Laura wondered whether anyone else would be out on this quiet road and could help if we got stuck. We got our answer a few minutes later when an SxS came roaring around a corner, scaring the bejeebers out of us and forcing us to pull into the tree branches on the right edge of the narrow road. Following this vehicle were 30 more, none of them slowing down in our presence. We continued and came to a flooded section of the road some SxS vehicles were wading through. We parked our car, got out, and walked.

Side-by-sides are modern-day dune buggies. In the 1960s, folks were taking VW Beetles, and shortening the chassis to create a dune buggy. These light, two-wheel vehicles had large wheels and high ground clearance, good traction, and could go almost anywhere. Mostly just to drive off-road, just for fun, not to go anywhere for a purpose. Most were not street legal. The buggies were built by individual enthusiasts, not by international companies like Yamaha and Kawasaki.

I constructed a dune buggy in the late 1960s after my family moved to Traverse City. I bought a shortened VW chassis and built up a dune buggy on top of it even before I had a driver's license. Building the buggy was a big part of my life for a few years. Because of the recent move, I had few friends. My mom would take me to the junkyard to get parts for the vehicle. I bought a Chilton's VW repair manual and learned how to work on the engine, brakes, and other components. The book became stained with oil as I used it regularly. Cars were much simpler back then, and more people did their own repairs. Besides, I had no money to take it to a mechanic.

Once I got the dune buggy up and running, I would access two-tracks at the Traverse City State Hospital grounds. For more far-reaching excursions, my mother, my sister Carol, or my brother Skip would drive our family car, towing the dune buggy. My friend Mike Street and I would go over to the sand dunes south of Esch Road in Leelanau County. We would camp for the weekend and run around on the dunes with a small group of older folks who owned more powerful dune buggies. A favorite activity was waterskiing behind the dune buggy as it ran along the beach. This was before these dunes became part of the Sleeping Bear National Lakeshore. The Park Service now prohibits all off-road vehicles, and even bicycles, from all but the gravel roads that are open to automobiles.

Access and transportation during the snowy winter months has also evolved in the north country. At Boggy's, we have seen snow over nine months of the year, so winter transport is not trivial. Original winter access was walking, by people and horses. A dog sled used to take mail up to Deer Park from Newberry. The transition between snow and no snow has always been a challenge, and still is. From a January 12, 1923, *Newberry News* article:

Automobiles have been operated with little difficulty so far this winter, the roads have been in fairly good condition. The storm yesterday, however, sent most of them to the garage until spring.

Imagine if the road commission told the public today that it was not going to plow the roads this winter, *"just park your car until spring"*?

The original snowmobiles were often just an early automobile, with skis on the front. Modern snowmobiles debuted in the 1950s. Because of the high snow depths along Lake Superior, winter can be the busiest time for restaurant and lodging establishments in these snow belt areas.

Isolation

We are acutely aware of the limited access and communication we have at Boggy's. We have no cell coverage, and it would only take a downed tree or deep pond in the road to force us to abandon our car and start walking. That is different on our winter trips. We ski in and are relying on human power to get into and out of the bush. We do not travel fast, but we can move safely and surely. We are prepared to travel no matter the elements, and we can go around a fallen tree or through a foot of new snow (which we have).

I have had one slight emergency where access to our car and open roads was appreciated. I was also glad I was not at Boggy's alone. Back in the early 1990s, I was installing new stove pipes for the sauna. For one of the pipes, I had to cut the length in half to fit. I only had some small tin snips, so I left a jagged end. I was trying to force this end into another pipe. As I wrestled with it, the jagged end slipped and cut my face. Somehow it missed my nose but cut a nice two-inch slash across my cheek. I sat down on the walkway next to the sauna and bled and bled. Laura came out and thought I was dying. The bleeding slowed down. We loaded the kids and dog in the car, and Laura drove to Newberry. Helen Newberry Joy Hospital had a physician assistant on duty. He said he could stitch me up, or we could drive to Marquette for a plastic surgeon. I told the PA to go for it. When I had the stitches removed a week later, my doctor (and friend) John Van Dalson told others in his office that he *"didn't put in those stitches."*

My sweet mother, who suffered dementia in her later years, would often remark when she saw me, *"You can't see the scar anymore."* I knew she was just being nice, because she would not have remembered my accident, let alone the scar. The scar is still visible.

Recent efforts continue to improve access for motorized tourists to and through this remote area, making the area less "isolated." Road improvements can often be a double-edged sword. They're an improvement for people who want to drive fast and far on paved, free-flowing highways, but they degrade the environment and experience for those who may want to drive slowly, are walking or cycling, or for the animals that inhabit the area.

Alger County and the Pictured Rocks National Lakeshore considered paving the county road between Munising and Grand Marais in the late 1990s. This would extend a paved road along the Lake Superior shore. The national park took comments from the public. Some folks were for it, some against. Funding was appropriated, and the full length of the road was paved between the two towns in 2008–2010. The Luce County Road Commission is now considering extending this lakefront paved road easterly towards Deer Park. This project would bring another paved road and more traffic to the intersection where we get on graveled 410 to head east to Boggy's.

Within the Two Hearted watershed, the original 1973 Natural River Plan contemplated only access to fishing and hunting camps on two-tracks in pickup trucks or passenger cars. The plan did not envision packs of side-by-sides racing along logging roads and forest roads. As our lives become more and more dependent on warm, convenient motorized vehicles for access to everywhere we go, we do not think about what happens if our vehicle breaks down or encounters an obstruction. In much of the U.S., cell service can now deliver help with a simple phone call.

Remote areas like the Two Hearted watershed still have areas without cell service, and help is farther away. Here is a story of two local residents who were experienced with the road and weather conditions of this northern outpost but made fatal decisions.

IN MEMORIAM
Doctor Leslie E. Purman
Faye (Leighton) Purman

The Land They Loved
In the wet fall eve, they lost their way
And on this place exhausted lay.
While death's chill dew upon their brows
Turned frost with cold
The wild, swirling winds their requiem blew.
Drifting snow flakes their eyelids softly co'ering
They slept together in the Land They Loved.
November 27–28, 1966

A memorial plaque with these words is attached to a huge rock, a few hundred yards from Pine Stump Junction. We saw this plaque, and read the chilling poem, not long after we bought Boggy's Camp. Recently, we learned the rest of the story.

Faye Leighton had owned and operated Pike Lake Resort since 1941. In 1964, Faye married a longtime family friend, Leslie "Doc" Purman. The resort was located about 12 miles east of Pine Stump Junction. A November storm blew in off Superior. The last of the deer hunters had left the resort, and the Purmans were going to leave on Monday. Friends contacted them (through ham radios) and said they should leave right away, because the heavy rainstorm was going to turn to snow. They got in their car and drove west on County Road (CR) 412. They tried to drive through a deep puddle, and their car died. They had to walk.

They never showed up that night or the next day, and family and friends appealed to the Luce County Road Commission to plow the road to look for them. They first plowed into Pike Lake from the east from plowed CR 500. No car was found. The road commission then plowed CR 412 in from the west and found their empty car about four miles east of Pine Stump. The workers plowed the road wider to look for any trace of them, while helicopters searched for tracks, along with tracking dogs. On Monday, December 5, a week after they were reported missing, a friend of the Purmans was stationed at the intersection of CR 407 and 412 to keep other drivers off 412. Fresh scent could throw off the tracking dogs. As one of the friends was waiting, she explored a large spruce tree near the intersection, and found Ms. Purman under the branches of the tree. Mr. Purman was found about 10 feet away. They were 100 yards from safety.

I also learned of one other couple stranded during this same storm. I found this story while looking at old *Newberry News* editions on microfilm at the Tahquamenon Library. I was looking for more information on the Purmans, and so was searching the weekly paper around that date.

In the December 1, 1966, edition, there was a story about Jack and Jane Miller who were staying at Hunter's Camp on the Two Hearted. They were going to leave Sunday, but it was wet and raining hard. By Monday, the deep snow kept them from leaving. They wondered if anyone knew they were there. Camp owner Glen Hunter knew they were there and knew they would have trouble getting out. He and a friend tried to get back to the camp on Monday, but the storm thwarted their efforts. On Tuesday, they returned with a group of 12 snowmobiles and some chainsaws. They made their way back into the camp, plowing through snow drifts, and cutting up windblown trees. They rescued the Millers but did not get back to Newberry until 4:40 a.m. Wednesday morning.

There are many more stories of people stuck in this remote area. Long-time residents and business owners all have stories. Most of them result in an inconvenience, not loss of life.

Road Impacts to the Watershed

Roads allow easy access to wonderful places, but they do harm the forest, the flora and fauna, and water resources. Roads can fragment the forest and produce edge effects, changing the vegetation within the forest due to the opening. Motorized vehicle access also has direct impact on animals through physical injury and death. Motorized vehicles also emit noise which can lead to behavior changes in animals. Between snowmobiles and SxS vehicles, animals do not get a break from the stressful impacts of noise, affecting their ability to find food and avoid predators.

In 2006, the Luce County Board of Commissioners opened all Luce County roads to ORVs (off-road vehicles). This allowed greater access everywhere in the county, without trailering the ORVs. Every forest road, fire lane, or logging road was then accessible from the county roads. There were numerous public complaints and photos of ORV damage in the Two

Photos from 2008 Two Hearted Watershed Management Plan. *Source: Superior Watershed Partnership*

Hearted watershed, including tracks in wetlands, and fording streams. Illegal use not only threatens the environment, but it threatens future respectful ORV use. Law-abiding citizens may lose access rights if bad players continue to cause damage.

In response to the complaints, Luce County developed an educational campaign to reduce illegal and troublesome ORV use. The multiple forest roads in the watershed also provide access to Lake Superior dunes and beaches, where it is unlawful to travel in an ORV.

In 2022, officials limited ORV riding hours on public land during the rifle deer season. Virtually all the watershed is open to public hunting, so this was a significant closure.

> *To promote safety for anyone going out into the woods, some riding areas may be closed to ORVs and snowmobiles during firearm deer season.*
>
> *During these two weeks, ORVs and snowmobiles may not be operated between the hours of 7–11 am and 2–5 pm on any area open to public hunting. This also promotes "quiet hours" for wildlife.*

Roads interrupt natural stream flow. Even when roads and culverts are properly designed, lack of maintenance can cause excessive ponding upstream of the road, and erosion of soils on the downstream side. Corrugated steel pipe is used for stream crossings under roads. These pipes can shift and collapse, and do not allow the natural stream bottom to continue, and hence interrupt fish and macroinvertebrate migration. Based on the 2008 Two Hearted River Watershed Management Plan, efforts were launched to correct some of the trouble spots in the watershed and reconnect the tributaries.

> *Re-onnecting the Two Hearted River - A six-year effort has now been completed—using funds from EPA's Great Lakes Restoration Initiative and other sources—to reconnect 35 miles of the Two Hearted River. As a result, this waterway is now one of the longest free-flowing rivers in the Great Lakes.*
>
> *Though the Two Hearted is the only designated wilderness river in the state, that doesn't mean the watershed hasn't been beaten up, much of its bruising from sweeping white pine clear-cutting decades ago. More recently, stream crossings over culverts have collapsed, creating jams and resulting in sediment*

pouring into the waterway. The stream then fractured, with spawning beds smothering from siltation.

Emily Clegg worked on this project for the Nature Conservancy. The project implemented recommendations from the management plan that she had helped write.

I really had a sense of accomplishment when I went back to do post-construction monitoring and saw brook trout in places they hadn't been able to get to before.

ORV and Snowmobile Trails

The Two Hearted watershed is a Midwest snowmobile destination. MDNR Trail 8 is a west-east snowmobile trail that parallels Lake Superior and connects Grand Marais to the Two Hearted watershed, and then continues south to Tahquamenon State Park. Although remote from population centers, this is one of the state's most popular trails because it goes through one of the prime lake-effect snow areas. MDNR Trail 9 is a snowmobile trail that traverses from Newberry northeast up into the watershed. These two trails are part of a network of 3,000 miles of groomed snowmobile trails in the U.P. It is not unusual for 'bilers to ride hundreds of miles for food and beer, and then many more to get to their motel.

ORV trails extend and crisscross in a web of access through state land in the watershed. We have met people on the trails that live in Newberry, downstate Michigan, and as far away as Texas. Some are lost. Some are just friendly and stop to say "hi." Two MDNR ORV trails intersect at an ORV parking area on CR 407 just north of the river. The Pine Ridge ORV trail is a 47-mile-long looping trail west of CR 407. The trail connects to the Two Hearted ORV Trail which is east of 407. This is a 36-mile-long trail that connects to the mouth of the Two Hearted River. All county roads and public forest roads are open to ORV traffic except one—Pretty Lake Road.

The Two Hearted ORV Trail and the MDNR snowmobile Trail 8 both cross the main branch of the Two Hearted at the Reed and Green Bridge. Boggy's Camp is impacted by this traffic because of its proximity to this bridge. Boggy's is just a mile away, a short jaunt for curious riders. The isolated peninsula of state land located between the Two Hearted and Lake

Superior east of Boggy's seems to be a draw for the more adventurous. Mapping apps help with wayfinding. These folks go right through our property on Boggy's Camp Trail. Most are respectful; some are hell-bent on driving fast and kicking up dust.

A quiet evening in the dark of winter is rare because of the distant roar of snowmobiles travelling on Trail 8. Many snowmobiles are 4-cycle now instead of 2-cycle. This makes them much quieter.

Boggy's Camp Trail is a historic forest road that starts at the Reed and Green Campground, goes through our property, and then traverses north past the Coast Guard Road to Lake Superior. The trail was named some years back when all the cabins were identified with red number signs to help with emergency response. The Luce County Road Commission maintains CR 374 from CR 410 to the Reed and Green campground. They do not maintain Boggy's Camp Trail. The property owner that purchased the Lake Superior frontage north of us brought in load after load of gravel in the late 1990s to improve the road. This road provides access to the cabins and lots he subdivided on the big lake, along with a few other private parcels on the river and the Big Lake.

CHAPTER 13

PEOPLE-POWERED ACCESS

A man on foot, on horseback or on a bicycle will see more, feel more, enjoy more in one mile than the motorized tourist can in a hundred miles.

—**Edward Abbey,** *Desert Solitaire*

During the first decade of our family visits to Boggy's, we very seldom drove the car after arriving. We would go running, hiking, mountain biking, or canoeing, but the car would sit. Doing what we called the "*Boggy's Thing*" was a concerted effort to stay put. Although we did drive to Pictured Rocks and Tahquamenon Falls, canoed to the river mouth, and did some long runs and mountain bike rides, those were the exceptions. The goal was to not hurry through events and enjoy just being at Boggy's and its environs. Having no TVs and no cell phone coverage (when cell phones became a thing), has helped us live an uncomplicated life at Boggy's.

A typical vacation day at Boggy's when the girls were young began with coffee. I made a ritual of having my first cup on the bank, a sanctuary, with only a dog for company. After everyone stirred, the day proceeded with blueberry pancakes. Gathering the blueberries got us outside, where we would try to spend most of the day. Various folks would then go for a run, hike, or mountain bike, or play games. The girls would work on their

Claire, Annie, Julia, and Chester playing outside on a rainy day in 1993.

fort and I on the bank. In the afternoon, we would dip in the river or Lake Superior, canoe, heat up the sun shower, play cards, take a nap, and prepare dinner. Many short canoe rides would involve paddling upstream a way, surprising fishermen, and floating back down. In the evening, we would do the dishes, play cards, read, or hike to the big lake for the sunset. If cool, the adults might take a sauna before we all sat by the campfire. If it was warm, some of us might use the sun shower. Rainy days were enjoyed in the cabin, playing family card games, working on art projects, or reading. Family vacations are treasured time, best saved for August in the U.P. The big lake waters have warmed enough to swim, and the masses of mosquitos and black flies have passed.

Sometimes complications happen and mess up our ability to hunker down. Laura cut her finger when a glass broke washing dishes on a Sunday evening. We decided Monday to load the girls in the car and drive to Newberry for stitches.

We keep the canoe and two old mountain bikes at our cabin. We enjoy exploring the remote forests that surround our camp, and very seldom see another person when we are not on one of the county roads. These silent sports are less popular than motor sports. Anglers wandering along the river and the increase in hikers using the North Country Trail and camping at the Reed and Green State Forest Campground next door help expand the quiet culture.

Access to Boggy's in the winter on skis is an adventure all its own with a separate set of demands. The closest plowed road leaves about a five-mile ski into Boggy's. We find a parking spot off CR 407 and get skiing early in the day to get to the cabin with time to get it cleared of snow and warmed up. When the girls were small, I would pull in a sled to help carry additional gear and food. The girls would also carry their own backpacks. The nice thing about skiing into a cabin is that we leave some clothes and food in the fall to lighten our load.

No matter what the route, it is about a two-hour ski along forest and county roads, made easier on trails packed down by snowmobiles. Once we get to the cabin, we dig out the front door, and get inside to start a fire in the wood stove. We then need to dig out the propane tank, the well, the sauna, and the back door off the kitchen. We unpack the sled and backpacks and leave our jackets on until the cabin warms up. The cooking oil and dish soap don't flow until a few hours later, when the wood stove does its job.

Hiking
North Country Trail
When we bought Boggy's in 1991, the North Country Trail was marked and open and paralleled the Lake Superior shore, just north of our cabin. Boggy's Camp Trail connects the Reed and Green SFCG with Lake Superior. This was difficult to walk on because of the fragile soils, easily damaged and made sterile because of off-road vehicle use. To avoid the soft sand, we developed our own single-track hiking trail—utilizing some abandoned logging roads—that stretched from our camp to the NCT. The Coast Guard Road that goes east-west north of Boggy's is also very sandy and only passable by 4-wheel drive vehicles with high ground clearance.

The National Trails Systems Act of 1968 designated the existing Appalachian and the Pacific Crest Trails as the first national scenic trails. The North Country Trail, the longest of the national scenic trails, stretches 4,800 miles through eight states. The trail, begun in the late 1980s, connects North Dakota to Vermont. Michigan has the most mileage of any state with over 1,000 miles of trail. The North Country Trail in the U.P.

extends from Wisconsin, east along Lake Superior to the mouth of the Two
Hearted River, and then south through Tahquamenon Falls State Park to
St. Ignace.

Here is a journal entry from the fall of 2009. I had just given notice to
the TART Trails Board that I was leaving the organization. I had been the
Executive Director of the Traverse City based trails, bike, and walk advo-
cacy group for almost a decade.

> *I went for a walk to the Big Lake. I took the normal route—gravel road north,
> two-track east past the cabin, looked at the river from the ridge, then north
> towards the NCT. Weather was perfect, Jac was acting spry. We travelled over
> the dune ridges, blueberries plentiful on north slopes. When we got to the sec-
> tion that climbs and trends west, we set off to the northeast.*
>
> *I was looking for a new route, a different path. The destination was the
> same, but an untrampled variation lay ahead. We encountered an old two-
> track that I had been on 15 years ago when searching, still hoping for good
> mountain biking. We travelled east, then set off again north towards the lake.
> We climbed an open hill, the vegetation changed, and the horizon expanded
> over the Big Lake, expansive view, breathtaking. We scrambled down the sand
> bluff and sauntered west, slowly, along the shore.*
>
> **Boggy's Camp Journal, Bob, September 25, 2009**

Historically, the NCT dropped south to the Coast Guard Road north of
Boggy's to get around private property. In 2018, the NCT Association volunteers created a new single-track through the state forest, reducing the
sandy road walking. This new section of trail is much more picturesque and
enjoyable to walk. ORVs have access on MDNR forest roads to both ends
of this new section of trail. Volunteers have worked with the MDNR on
signage and have placed brush piles to try to stop them from accessing this
hiking trail, tearing up the fragile landscape, and creating new ORV trails
on the state land. The moss and lichen are easily destroyed, and the impact
is visible for years.

Laura and I recently adopted three miles of the North Country Trail
east of Boggy's. We walk the trail, trim back brush and tree limbs, and paint
blazes as needed for wayfinding. We are not certified to use a chainsaw to
cut up fallen trees. If we find a large tree that needs to be moved, we contact

Laura and Marta along the NCT with marking paint, May 2022.

folks from the Superior Shoreline Chapter of the NCT. This chapter helps maintain the NCT from the mouth of the Two Hearted all the way west to Munising.

The trail east and west of Boggy's has some beautiful sections, including elevated views of Lake Superior from rolling hills of red and white pine. This section, due to its proximity to bluffs along Lake Superior, has been rerouted several times away from the lake as erosion has cut into the bluffs. It is not unusual to see trees marked with the blue NCT blazes lying on the bluff. Our adopted three-mile section ends at the western edge of where the Duck Lake Fire hit the beach.

Fisherman Trail

Any good trout stream will have a path trampled along it where anglers walk to search out places to fish. The Two Hearted near Boggy's is such a stream. The high spring flows keep anglers out of the river and on the bank. These paths are more visible where there is vehicle access to the river at road crossings or campgrounds. We often hike along the river near Boggy's, with good views of the river.

Mountain Biking

During our early visits to Boggy's, I did a fair amount of exploring on my mountain bike. Laura and I had small children so we would walk as a family as far as we could. Individually, Laura might then do a run and I would do a bike ride for escape and exercise. I would explore far and wide with only a compass and USGS quadrangle maps for directions. Many of the old logging roads on the maps were accessible. I encountered very few people, and little evidence of development of any kind. Occasionally, I found an old camp out in the woods or on the river. Sometimes the camp had evidence of recent visits, sometimes not. The remoteness of these rides was often exhilarating, sometimes scary.

The negative impact of ORVs has increased on these small, isolated two-tracks. Some of the formerly green, mossy two-tracks have become rutted roads with soft sand and poor access for anything other than a high clearance, four-wheel drive vehicle. Two-tracks were so named because grass would grow between the wheel marks because of infrequent vehicle use. The spacing between the two-tracks has been a consistent width, set by the average automobile. The ATVs now have a narrower footprint and can more easily tear up the vegetation in the middle. Two-tracks are disappearing from the watershed.

The deteriorating access for bicycles in the watershed is ironic because cyclists were the first ones who asked for better roads in Michigan in the late 1800s. The first director of the Michigan State Highway Department was a cyclist, Horatio S. "Good Roads" Earle. Earle was the president of the League of American Wheelmen in 1901. LAW was a national organization that advocated for cyclists during the cycling boom of the 1880s to 1890s (now named League of American Bicyclists). Earl eventually became the first director of the newly formed State Highway Department in 1905. Not everyone approved of the effort to improve the road surface, including Henry Ford and farmers who did not want more traffic in their quiet rural areas. From the *Michigan Highways* website:

> *The distinguished automobile pioneer, Henry Ford, gave little support to the good roads movement. He believed that his automobiles, especially the famous Model T, not only could withstand any kind of road conditions, but that roads required only minimal improvements to make auto travel passable.*

Ford could not have envisioned the number of cars his innovative manufacturing methods would produce, nor America's appetite for them. Some soils that can survive with light traffic, quickly deteriorate with more.

Current SUV television ad campaigns promote "everywhere access" and show vehicles smashing through walls of snow on mountain roads, fording rivers, and travelling through narrow forest roads. The Ford Motor Company promotes their "Adventurous Bronco" with 300 horsepower, 35-inch all-terrain tires, high ground clearance, and an air intake located such that the vehicle can go through 36 inches of water. Other than mature trees or a metal gate, few things can stop this vehicle. Ironically, the terrain that SUVs spend most of their time on is smooth asphalt.

My daughter Claire and I travelled by bike to Boggy's when she was in college. We rode our mountain bikes and pulled a trailer with camping equipment. We needed mountain bikes for the last 15 miles on gravel roads. We left Traverse City and camped at the Petoskey City Campground the first night. Straits State Park in St. Ignace was the next overnight, and then Tahquamenon Falls State Park. We then travelled up gravel county roads to Pike Lake, and then over to Boggy's.

Bob with trailer, Traverse City to Boggy's Camp bike tour. At the intersection of County Road 500 and 414, 2001.

This was the only time we cycled up to Boggy's; afterwards we got a ride home from Laura and the other girls. We have some guilt owning a cabin 200 miles from our home. In general, we try to live car light. Our family has had only one car for the past 30 years, and we live near downtown Traverse City. This enables us to walk and bike for most of our trips around town. But when we go to Boggy's, we drive to get there. We are already contemplating how we get to Boggy's when we buy an electric car. Battery charging is extremely limited in Luce County.

Canoeing

During our summer 1996 vacation, Claire, Annie, and I did a short canoe up the river. We pulled the canoe up onto the shore upstream of Boggy's and went in for lunch. We came out later that afternoon and the canoe was gone, out of sight. Panic hit. We went down to the shore to look around. Fortunately, the canoe was spotted bobbing up and down at the far bend of the river, caught on a branch. There was an old inflatable fisherman donut in the bunk room that I grabbed and floated down the river with a paddle. I got in the canoe, and paddled back up to the girls, waiting on the shore. The canoe was rescued, and I was a mini hero. We wrote our name and phone number inside the canoe after that.

The original access to the watershed was by water. Lake Superior provided access to ships and boats along the shore, and to the mouth of the Two Hearted. Before that, Native Americans plied the waters of the big lake, and travelled up the river in canoes looking for the flora and fauna that they survived on.

Canoe access continued through the 1900s, interrupted by the log drives of the late 1800s and early 1900s. Pike Lake Resort, close to the river mouth, was established in the 1940s and rented canoes. Rainbow Lodge, located at the mouth, opened in the 1960s. The lodge had a busy canoe livery business until 2012 when the Duck Lake Fire wiped out the business.

Most canoeing happens on the 11-mile-long section of river between the Reed and Green Bridge and the mouth. Canoe and kayak traffic on the river appears to have declined over the past 10 years. Kayaks are now the most frequent watercraft on the river past our camp. Some folks are fishing as they go by, some with coolers and a cold beer in their hand. Canoe

Claire, Julia, and Annie, headed to mouth of Two Hearted River, 2004.

and kayak trespassing has caused complaints on some Northern Michigan rivers. We have enjoyed our interactions with people as they pass our place. The silent crafts do worry us when we occasionally skinny dip when taking a sauna.

The 10-mile section from the High Bridge (CR 407) to the Reed and Green Bridge (CR 410) is lightly used because of numerous log jams that one must lift over or portage around. Laura and I have canoed this section twice and will not again. There is an old canoe camp about two thirds of the way down this section. The camp is now unreachable by vehicle, but I have found a way there via an old two-track on my mountain bike.

Laura and I first canoed this stretch in 1991, the first autumn we bought Boggy's. Laura was 7 months pregnant, and for good measure, we brought our 80-pound dog Chester. We had a copy of Jerry Dennis and Craig Date's informative book, *Canoeing Michigan Rivers*. Laura bought me the book for my 36th birthday. For this stretch of the Two Hearted the book states *"not recommended for a casual trip."* We must not have remembered the small print and we were unprepared for the number of obstacles. I can still see Laura and Chester trying to balance on a narrow log as I yanked the canoe over the umpteenth hurdle we had met. This was before we recorded adventures in Boggy's Camp Journal, so the firsthand accounts are missing, but the mental pictures remain. We were on a remote river, no other humans within miles, and no cell phone. Youth can be oblivious to potential danger.

Other than the river, there is a nice series of lakes in the watershed, set up for canoe camping. The Pretty Lake Quiet Area does not allow motorized boats and has a primitive campground accessible by a short stretch of county road. The one-mile-long access road is the only Luce County Road that prohibits ORVs. There are several lakes in the quiet area connected with short portages, and a few backcountry campsites.

CHAPTER 14

SPORTSMEN— CAMPS AND SERVICES

The first permanent buildings built in the watershed after the life saving station were the fishing and hunting camps, and the bars and stores that served them. The improving roads and new bridges allowed access. There were only a few dozen camps shown along the Two Hearted River and tributaries in the 1984 *Mapbook of Michigan Counties*. The *Mapbook* was based on 1934 base maps and has been updated regularly; however, updating of the recreational camps appears to have stopped in the 1950s.

Near our camp, the *Mapbook* shows three historic camps: Boggy's, Beeches, and Two Hearted. Lone Pine Camp was the only camp shown upstream between the Reed and Green Bridge and the High Bridge. I have visited this location on my bicycle, and no cabin remains.

Our closest neighbor, Beeches Camp, is about 400 feet away as the crow flies. Via canoe it is downstream around two bends of the river. Former U.S. Senator William Saxbe of Ohio previously owned this camp. He bought it in the 1960s. Saxbe vacationed and spent summers near Newberry starting in his boyhood in the 1920s. In 1969, Saxbe was Newberry's Fourth of July Parade Grand Marshal. As a U.S. senator in 1972, he is quoted in an encyclopedia.com article, commenting on Nixon's professed innocence in the Watergate scandals. Saxby said that Nixon sounded *"like the fellow who played the piano in a brothel for twenty years and insisted that he didn't know what was going on upstairs."* No hard feelings, because Saxby became President Nixon's fourth Attorney General, nominated in 1973, and then became President Ford's Attorney General when Nixon resigned.

Farther downstream, the Two Hearted Camp is still there, owned by the Two Hearted Club. There are also a few nearby camps not shown on the *Mapbook*. A nice small cabin built maybe in the 1980s is located on the river just east of Beeches Camp. This cabin was never finished on the inside, and we have never seen anyone there. We often walk an abandoned two-track that passes it.

Pea-Brain Camp is located in the woods on the Coast Guard Road, just north of Boggy's. This camp was built in the 1980s by two local men. We met Pea and Brain when they were having their annual pig roast for friends. Our dog Chester was delighted when he found a pile of bones stacked near the ground.

Another nearby camp, the closest one upstream of us, is located high above the river on High Banks Trail. The camp is located about one mile away from Boggy's as the crow flies, but is over two river miles away. We have tried to paddle upstream to this camp but have always been turned back by multiple log jams upstream of Reed and Green Bridge. This camp was built in the 1950s and a series of folks from the Traverse City area, including Paul Williams, have owned it. Paul told me when he first visited the camp to consider purchasing that there were many maps covering the wood paneling inside; he asked about the maps and learned the rest of the story. A couple who formerly owned the camp got divorced. The disgruntled husband, who lost the camp to his wife, came back to the camp one day, opened the door, and shot out all the propane lights with a shotgun. The maps were hiding the buckshot scars. The scars are still there.

Hundreds of Chippewa Hunters Ready for Annual 'Great Adventure' in Deer Woods. Many Camps in County to be Opened During the Weekend. The Evening News (Sault Ste. Marie, Michigan), November 11, 1939

*There will be a hum of activity in scores of camps in the eastern Upper Penin-
sula this weekend as a record-breaking crowd of hunters make preparations for
the opening of the deer season November 15.*

*Hunters were keeping a wary eye on the weather, trusting that a nice snow-
fall, the greatest blessing a deer hunter can ask, will be forthcoming before
Wednesday. Headquarters for most of the Sault and Chippewa county hunts-
men are shown on the map above . . .*

*Boggy's camp. Fred Shafer, Archie Larkin, Sherwin Overholt, Vernon Ai-
kens, Fred Young of Newberry, Stewart Blain and Joe Rogers will be at the
camp on the Two Hearted river. They expect to leave Monday night.*

A November 10, 1922, story in the Newberry News describes the influx of
hunters just before Michigan's deer season. Many hunters arrived with their
gear on trains at Mackinaw City, St. Ignace, and Soo Junction in the 1920s.
"States represented on the train leaving Detroit for the Upper Peninsula
Monday night were: Minnesota, Ohio, Illinois, Indiana, Wisconsin, and
Massachusetts," the *Newberry News* reported. As roads improved and autos
proliferated, sportsmen switched to driving "Up North."

East Branch Sportsmen's Club

The East Branch Sportsmen's Club and the Spile Dam Club along the East
Branch have hosted people camping and hunting as early as the 1920s. The
EBSC was established in 1937 by Harry Potter so land could be purchased.
The first property was bought in 1938, a total of 1,675 acres at a price of
$2.50/acre. About 50 members were asked to join.

Some of the existing cabins were from the logging camp (Webster
Lumber Company) that formerly owned and occupied the land. The cabin
construction is similar throughout the club, many having steel roofs and
rolled roofing sides. The rolled roofing discourages porcupines from nib-
bling and provides nice subtle colors to the cabins.

The EBSC is still going strong, with a full-time live-in caretaker during
three seasons. There are 60 members, 20 members each from three different regions of lower Michigan: Flint, Battle Creek, and Milan. On Labor
Day weekend, 2022, they had a picnic with 100 attendees. The EBSC now
owns 4,005 acres.

There are six gates on the property, five of them locked. The main gate is unlocked and has a sign-in sheet at the entrance. Upon invite, Laura and I visited Bill Knapp, the president of the club, in September 2022. Bill and his wife, Lorine, have a nice cabin, with all the comforts of home. Solar panels and propane power the cabin, which has running water, a stove, a refrigerator, and heat. Bill's father joined the club in 1954, so Bill has been coming here since he was a kid.

In October I went back to the EBSC to meet the caretaker, Keith King. We got in his side-by-side and toured the property. There are about 30 miles of roads and trails on the property. We drove south to the Spile Dam Club property. The SDC is allowed access through the EBSC main gate. Many of the cabins at both clubs are not on the banks of the East Branch, but some distance away.

Caretaker's cabin, East Branch Sportsmen's Club, 2022.

Keith had only been the caretaker for a year but had been coming up to the area since he was two months old. His family has a camp across the East Branch, accessible through the EBSC property. There is now only one bridge across the East Branch on the property; there used to be another bridge on the Shamrock Road. This road led to a two-story camp they called the "Mansion." Henry Ford, Harvey Firestone, and Thomas Edison visited this camp back in the early 1900s. Those former captains of industry really got around. Reports of their visits are all over Northern Michigan and the U.P. This camp is gone now—burned down—but their legends remain.

Spile Dam Club

Harry's brother Everett Potter along with Cecil May founded the Spile Dam Club. Agnes Potter's Diary (Everett's wife) describes some of the early adventures of the founders of these two clubs, stretching back into the 1920s. The club was formed in 1934 with the purchase of 160 acres, for $3.50/acre. The club is located just upstream of the EBSC. There were 10 initial shareholders, and they built their first cabin in 1937.

Pine Stump Junction and Winter Haven Motel

Pine Stump Junction, located on CR 407, was initially just a postal address. During the height of the lumber camps, mail would be delivered from Newberry and set on a large pine stump. Loggers would come in from surrounding camps and receive and drop off mail.

Pine Stump Junction is also the name of a bar that has been there for 100 years. The bar has been open and serving drinks and food since we purchased Boggy's. Their busy season is winter when packs of snowmobiles stop by. We have seen dozens lined up in front, but have heard reports of as many as 100 snowmobiles congregated there. These days, we also see large groups of side-by-sides parked out front.

Initially the bar, located next to a small creek, was called Stagger Inn. Customers would keep their whiskey bottles in the creek to keep them cold. The creek is a tributary to Dawson Creek and is named Whiskey Creek.

Just north of the bar is the Winter Haven Motel, whose first four units were completed in 1986. Two more units were added in the early 1990s, and now there are eight units.

Rainbow Lodge

Rainbow Lodge, located close to the mouth of the Two Hearted River, was built in the mid 1960s, and burned down in 2012 in the Duck Lake Fire.

The lodge was built by Robby and Jean Robinson, and was owned and operated by their son Richard and his wife, Kathy, since the 1970s. The lodge name came from the beautiful colors of the area trout.

The lodge had a convenience store, a café for a few years, a motel and cabins, and an airstrip. Two of the cabins survived the fire, and since then four new cabins were built on a ridge across the road. The view of the big lake from this ridge was opened up by the fire.

Wolf Inn and North Store

About five miles south of Pine Stump is the historic Wolf Inn. The inn shows up on the early *Mapbook*. This restaurant has been open intermittently for the past 30 years since we have been coming to the area.

Across the street from the Wolf Inn is the North Store. This convenience store and gas station is owned by Larry and Tara Johnson. I got to know Larry when he installed the metal roof on our camp in 2017. Canoes, kayaks, ATVs, snowmobiles, and cabins can be rented at the North Store.

Deer Park Lodge

Deer Park was a lumber town in the late 1800s, and a former Native American encampment. Muskallonge Lake was a mill pond for logs brought to the lake by horses, and a railroad connected to Newberry. There is still a pile of sawdust on the Lake Superior frontage of Muskallonge State Park. There was also a life saving station, built in the 1870s. A post office and a school were at Deer Park for many years when the lumber camp was thriving.

Many private cottages sit on the east end of Muskallonge Lake, along with Deer Park Lodge, a convenience store, and cabin rental. The lodge was built by Robby and Jean Robinson in 1953. Robby had returned from the Korean War and was looking to get away from it all. They bought the land in 1952 and moved their family there in 1953. Their son Richard says he *"crossed the Straits of Mackinaw in 1953 when he was 6 weeks old, and never went back."*

The folks that own and operate Deer Park Lodge are the de facto mayors of the region; how is the fishing, how much snow is there, how are the mosquitos? These are just some of the services offered by remote stores.

Deer Park and Muskallonge Lake are not within the Two Hearted watershed, but just north of it.

Pike Lake Resort

Pike Lake, located just east of the Two Hearted watershed, had its first cabin in 1929. Claude and Faye Leighton purchased the land in 1930. They built Pike Lake Resort in the 1930s. Following Claude's death in 1941, Faye took over the resort until her untimely death in 1966.

From *The History of Pike Lake, 2000.*

Faye Leighton could do anything a man could do. She could repair her auto, operate a ham radio, was a skilled carpenter, and a capable card player. Faye drove a team of horses, drove a truck, and built a series of buildings. Faye swore, expectorated, argued, and told off-color stories and tall tales. She was a competent woman of the woods as she enjoyed fishing and hunting in the waters and forests of Luce County.

After Faye's death, the resort remained open until the Duck Lake Fire in 2012.

Campgrounds

Muskallonge Lake State Park is the largest campground in the area with 150 campsites. The campground was established in 1956. The campsites are on the north side of Muskallonge Lake. The park also has frontage on and hiking access to Lake Superior. Hikers on the NCT traverse a section of the campground and shoreline. The state park is an important source of customers for Deer Park Lodge, as are the surrounding camps.

The Two Hearted River State Forest Campground is located down the hill from the former Rainbow Lodge at the river mouth. There are 36 tent sites, in two different areas, separated by the day-use parking. A pedestrian bridge crosses the river to access Lake Superior. On the narrow spit of land between the river and the Big Lake, remains of the former life saving station still exist. This is a busy campground with anglers, canoers, and rockhounds. The NCT also goes through this campground.

Just 500 feet west of Boggy's is the Reed and Green State Forest Campground. This is our next-door neighbor, and we have enjoyed time spent with campers that have stayed there through the years. We have exchanged stories, food, and drinks with these folks, who are mostly from downstate Michigan. We have encountered former Boggy's Camp owner Jim and his sons camping there, along with several visitors who have made this camping spot an annual tradition. Many camp in small tents, some are in camper trailers, and one repeat visitor has a large canvas tent with a little wood stove. When driving into our camp, we play a game and guess *"how many campers will there be?"*

Other campgrounds in the watershed include the popular Pretty Lake SFCG, Holland Lake SFCG, Headquarters Lake Equestrian SFCG, and Perch Lake SFCG.

BOGGY'S CAMP

Peace by A.M. Rockwood, September 2020. Wood cut print based on artist Andy Rockwood's sketch made when he and his wife Laura spent a few days at Boggy's.

CHAPTER 15

THE CAMP

When we bought Boggy's in 1991, we got an old cabin, with the foundation timbers sitting on blocks. It looked like the cabin was piecemealed together over two or three stages. First the main cabin, then maybe the bunk room was added, then the kitchen, and small bathroom. The peaked roof over the bunk room had a big sag. We worried about that with the huge snow loads, and we were always glad to see it still standing when we skied in. The sag did not seem to get worse, but as time passed, the rolled roofing aged, and we knew a new roof was in our future.

We hired a local contractor, Larry Johnson, to build a new roof in 2017. He recommended building a new superstructure, to steepen the flatter roof sections over the kitchen, and support the sag. This seemed like a big job for one person, but Larry worked mostly alone, with occasional help from his dad or a friend. Steel roofing was laid on top.

Of course, the camp had a nice sauna (all U.P. camps have one). The sauna wood stove worked fine and was easy to get it cranking to get the sauna up to temperature. A few years ago, we were in the sauna and the red glow from the fire could be seen reflected off the floorboards. The bottom of the sauna had rusted through. Leo Nippa started making sauna stoves about 90 years ago in the U.P., following Finnish traditions. The company

(Nippa) has since moved to Beulah, Michigan. We found the perfect stove there and have been enjoying this new stove without worries of burning the sauna down (or camp, or surrounding forest).

An old equipment shed filled with antique tools, some red squirrel nests, and a generator came with the cabin. The large propane-powered generator was noisy and did not fit with the simple quietness of the setting. The water pump and many lights were all electric. We did not like to use the generator, so we got rid of it within the first year. Losing the generator, we lost running water, electric lights, and the use of a vacuum cleaner. We drilled a small diameter well by hand and installed a hand pump. Without running water, we must bucket flush the indoor toilet and fill containers for drinking and washing water. We also got rid of a hot water heater. The old electric lights are still hanging. I think they add a certain ambience. There was musty wall-to-wall carpeting we ripped out to expose lovely wood flooring that we can sweep.

The bunk room, moved to Boggy's from one of the old CCC camps, still has four sets of double bunk beds. We converted the two bunks in the entryway to a bench to let more light in. A perfect perch for Marta to keep track of anything passing by. The kitchen had a propane refrigerator (since gone), and has a propane stove. The camp also had a propane heater in the bunk room (gone) and still has a wood-burning stove for heat, and five propane lights.

We removed a small second stove from the kitchen. Our firewood supplier Greg had brought us some wood and he was interested in the stove for his camp on a Tahquamenon tributary. Before we knew it, Greg picked up the stove and carried it, by himself, to his truck. He took it so fast we did not have time to remove some blueberry buckle and potatoes we were storing in the stove. He told us later he enjoyed them.

In the winter, when we cannot use the indoor plumbing, we would build a toilet out of snow. The structure could barely survive a few days of use, so we built a permanent "slammer" for winter use. We learned of these in the Boundary Waters canoe area. They are open air outhouses, just a seat, never stinky. In the Boundary Waters, they are located distant from the backcountry tent sites for privacy. The slam is to let others in your party know you are done. At Boggy's, we initially put our slammer out past the sauna, with a view of the river. It now sits near our east property line, with a pleasing view of the woods.

The indoor toilet connects to a septic tank/drain field. We left water in the tank one autumn, and it froze, and the ice broke the toilet tank in half. The toilet still works, if flushed by a bucket. We very seldom use the sink in the bathroom—it still empties into a bucket. The door to the small bathroom is in a back corner of the bunk room. We have had guests stay at Boggy's that never saw the bathroom. They just used the slammer, and assumed we were just kidding about the inside toilet. For some reason, the kitchen sink was originally plumbed to a standpipe off the kitchen. We re-plumbed the sink to the septic system.

> *Dear Boggy's Notebook,*
>
> *My name is Eric. I came here yesterday with Bob and Jac. On the way here we stopped at the grocery store in Newberry & bought food. It was fun to shop with Bob. Jac waited in the car. Then we stopped at the Wolf Inn. Then we stopped at Pine Stump Junction. We finally got to Boggy's at 6:30, but only after Bob took the time to show me where two people froze to death—thanks Bob for sharing that with me. We had excellent chili that Laura made for dinner. We had great pancakes for breakfast. Then we started to dig up the old sewer line from the kitchen sink! We dug & dug & dug half-way down to the river until the pipe entered a secret chamber. Excitedly we opened the lid and found . . . 55 gallons of Boggy's sludge. We quickly buried it back up and walked to Lake Superior. Bob still smells like sludge! I caught a big fish. Boggy's is a very nice place.*
>
> **Eric Gerstner, October 12, 2000**

Eric is a former neighbor, friend, and importantly, is very handy. Boggy's had a Formica kitchen countertop with duct tape patches. Laura was not enamored with it. With Eric in charge, we took measurements, and then back home we purchased southern yellow pine, cut it to size and glued it together. We finished it with several coats of polyurethane and took it back up to Boggy's in two sections. The new countertop fit like a glove, and we have enjoyed it ever since.

In addition to the cabin, we also received *chattel* with our purchase, a word I had not heard before. The chattel includes those things not part of the cabin or outbuildings: old furniture, old dishes and silverware, pots and pans. These are all things we would have had to buy if we had bought land to build a cabin—and what we bought would have had less character. We are still using most of these items and have grown attached to the ugly, light green matching plates, and the cast iron skillets. One U.P. camp rule we try to follow is to bring *nothing new* to the camp.

We also received a few special things: Boggy's World War I duffle, a felt-topped poker table, a handmade 30-inch-long cribbage board, and nameplates to label the bunks. When Boggy had friends up to the camp, he had wooden nameplates for each person. He would put their name on a specific bunk for use that visit. We still have a name tag for Boggy and Charles. Not sure who Charles was, but Boggy's and Charles's name tags were on a bunk bed in a little vestibule right where you walk in the front door. Perhaps Charles was a beloved dog.

We also received something we did not want—broken glass. Decades of beer and whiskey bottles had been pitched over the riverbank. We have found a few nice old bottles, but mostly glass shards. We clean them up, and then the next year some new ones work their way up from the bank.

Boggy's is remote, no neighbors, no cell phone service, no automobile access for half of the year. We enjoy this isolation and hope that cell service never reaches us. Over the past decade, new towers have been built near Pine Stump and Tahquamenon State Park. Cell service still fails to reach us. We do have a good radio at the camp, however. The radio receives AM, FM, and weather. We get two FM stations: Oldies (WNBY) out of Newberry, and depending on the weather, an NPR station out of Sault Ste. Marie.

Boggy's cabin has never been vandalized. Sometimes we come inside the cabin after a few months away and wonder if things are different than we left them. Did one of the past visitors have a key and stay for a few days? We did have a window broken once. A hawk flew into one of the dining room windows on the river side. We only know this because an angler was there and heard/saw it. He reported the problem to Mike and Monica at Deer Park Store, and they made sure the window was fixed to keep the varmints out. U.P. kindness in action.

CHAPTER 16

CAMP DOGS

U.P. camps require not only a sauna, but also a camp dog. We have had three who all enjoyed being at camp more than at our home in Traverse City. First off, no leashes or fences. Also, I think the many smells are new and exhilarating for them in the north woods of the U.P. And finally, our family policy was no dogs on beds or furniture at home. This policy was broken because there was already a Boggy's tradition of the dogs sleeping on the bunk labelled Charles, the first lower bunk when you walk in the cabin.

Chester was our first camp dog. He was seven when we bought Boggy's and he spent some quality time there. We got Chester the first year we were married, and he was a good dog. People say you only get one good dog. He was well trained because I was in graduate school when we got him, so I had flexible time. We spent many hours together. I knew a barber whose passion was duck hunting. He would get a group of us together with our retriever puppies for training. Chester grew into an 80-pound black Lab. He would faithfully follow the important commands: sit, stay, come. He could also do blind retrieves, useful and humane for duck hunting, because often the hunter will see where the duck falls, but the dog does not see it. I could

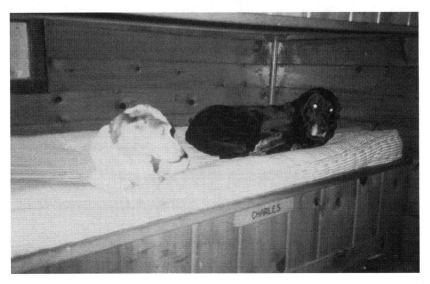

Chester and Seph relaxing on Charles's bunk.

blow a whistle, Chester would look at me, and I would give him directional hand signals to finish the retrieve.

Next came Jac. His name was spelled with the first initials of our three daughters. He was a big, good looking, happy black Lab with an insatiable appetite. And he was naughty his whole life.

Jac was enthusiastic and strong. He pulled Laura down during puppy training, pulled Julia across the grass while watching a sister's soccer game, and devoured 10 pounds of the kids' Halloween candy and survived with only a bad bout of diarrhea. As a puppy at Boggy's, he chased the three girls up to the top bunks when Laura and I were out for a short run. He is the only dog that journeyed the 500 feet down Boggy's Camp Trail to the Reed and Green State Forest Campground, alone, to enjoy a meal with some of the campers. We could never feed him enough.

> *Bob, Jac, and I came up late Tuesday and will head home tomorrow morning (Sunday). Yes, at 15 years, Jac is still coming to Boggy's. Hard to say how much longer, but he enjoys wandering around the camp, sniffing the wild unfamiliar smells, and just being with us . . . and of course eating, Jac still has a good appetite . . .*

Boggy's Camp Journal, Laura, May 14, 2013
(Note: Jac passed away on June 8, 2013)

Next came Marta, born in 2015, and still enjoying herself on walks in the north country. She is our first female dog, is a 40-pound mutt, but has Lab eating tendencies. In October 2018 I was visiting my neighbor Tom who has a cabin on Lake Superior. I had Marta with me, so Tom said wait, he would go upstairs and pick up some rat poison he had sitting on the floor so Marta would not get into it. We then proceeded to enjoy a beer and conversation when we heard a plastic bag rattling near the front door. Marta had her head inside a whole bag of rat poison pellets. I was not sure she got anything, but her instincts are to swallow things quickly. A trip to Newberry and $72 later, the vet had Marta puking out an undigested green pellet of poison.

Her stomach got her in trouble on another occasion while visiting Boggy's. Laura and I were walking with her and took a two-track towards the river. We looked down and Marta had fishing line hanging out of her mouth. The line disappeared into the back of her throat. It was Sunday and we were leaving that morning, so once we got cell phone service, we called around looking for an open vet office. There were 24-hour emergency vets in Manistique and Traverse City. We drove home and took her to the emergency vet hospital a few blocks from our home. They x-rayed her and saw a fishhook in her stomach. They kept her overnight and fed her some high fiber foods to see if she could pass it. The next day surgery was scheduled because the hook had not moved. The vet did one more x-ray before surgery and saw the hook had moved to her intestines. They suggested we take her home, feed her some more special food, and keep an eye on her stool. We were so excited when Laura found a fishhook, still in a spawn sack, when digging through her poop the next day.

CHAPTER 17

BOGGY'S CAMP JOURNAL

Our camp dogs were not the only animals that have shared the cabin with us. Mice have also been our guests—or are we theirs? As anyone who has a cabin in the woods knows, it is hard to keep field mice out in the field. Boggy's Camp has no foundation, just timbers sitting on concrete blocks. Previous owners did a respectable job putting a sheet metal skirt around the cabin, but it was not enough.

On August 30, 1997, we got here and then had dinner. We had hot dogs. Then we read for a long time then Claire and I made a mouse trap. It would not kill the mouse, but they would get stuck. It had a ramp going up to a 5-gallon bucket and in the bucket was cheese and crackers. We put crackers on the ramp too. Then we went to bed. In the morning the mice only ate the food on the ramp. They were probably scared to jump in. We went and picked blueberries then had blueberry pancakes. . . .

Then we went canoeing. Us kids didn't want to go at first, but then we had a lot of fun. Me and Claire got to paddle all the time we went downstream. We kept bumping into things. Then we played hearts. Then we got packed up and left.

Boggy's Camp Journal, Annie, 11, August 30, 1997

We are fortunate to have a written record of our activities at Boggy's over the past thirty years. Now on the third volume of Boggy's Camp Journal, we have a treasured record of our three daughters' maturation in writing, from first drawing in the journal before they could write, to some of their first journal posts. Below is a letter written to Laura and I by Claire. We had skied in to Boggy's with our 11-year-old Lab, Chester. This was written before we started our journal later that same year. Following Claire's letter are journal entries from Annie and Julia, also from our annual ski into the camp:

To Mommy and Daddy,
How is boggys going are you having fun here? I am having fun. I can't wait intil we go outside and make a snow hose. Do you think Chester will be able to make it home? He will probably need some goodnight sleeps. I woner what Annie and Julia are doing at home? I hope they are having a lot of fun at bubbys and papas house. I hope we have a lot of fun here.

Claire, 8, February 20, 1995

We went to a hotle before we came to Boggy's. This is the first time that I have come to Boggy's without Chester. This is my first time skiing up to Boggy's to. Claire and I made a fort outside and when we standup nobody can see us. There is 3 feet of snow here at Boggy's. Daddy and mommy shoveled snow off the roof and Claire and I helped by slideing up and down on the roof.

Annie, 7, March 9, 1996

I had a lot of fun when I went to Boggy's. Annie Claire and I went to our fuort and got all wet it was fun. When we got all wet we went to a log and took off our close and diride them off. We thout that we were going to get itrubell but we didn't.

Mommy and Daddy were going on a ski and Annie Claire and I played tripell solitar. And I read a lot. We read mistereys and othe stuff

I had a good time up hear too. We got to eat gorp.

Julia, 8, March 5, 2000

Llegamos el 19 de Octubre en medio de la oswridad. Fue' un viaje muy largo. Todo se veia negro, Mami y Papi nos preparon la cama, nos dispusimos a dormir, yo estaba ausustada ya que no sabia donde estaba y todo estaba muy oscuro . . . (Translation: We arrived on October 19 in the middle of darkness. It was a very long trip. Everything looked black, Mommy and Daddy prepared our bed, we got ready to sleep, I was scared because I didn't know where I was and everything was very dark.)

Rosana, October 20, 1996

Rosana was an exchange student from Colombia. She spoke and wrote well in English, but we asked her for a Spanish entry. We have stayed in touch, with Rosana returning to Traverse City with her family, and us visiting Rosana in Colombia.

Then some later journal entries, as the girls fly the coop.

I just got back from a great run and dip with Jac and now we're all eating Cheerios before heading out. It has been a wonderful trip with the best weather ever—it has been beautiful, sunny and pleasant! We did the classic Boggy's activities—going to Lake Superior, playing cards, riding bikes, running, reading, and relaxing.

On Saturday morning, while on a walk on Boggy's Trail, I got attacked by paper wasps and got stung on my neck, head and arm 5 times. It was scary!

This is my last trip up here before heading off to college in less than two weeks, so I am feeling very excited and nervous, and this is a great place to relax. This has been a great trip up here and I'm looking forward to coming back!

Annie, August 13, 2006

Annie and I came up for a long weekend with friends from school. She brought Matt and I invited Woodsy, Uible, Mark and Jeff. We killed a couple hundred Chinese beetles inside the cabin with duct tape. That was pretty fun.

Woodsy & I went for a good canoe trip early yesterday morning & we all spent the afternoon @ Lake Superior today. We played crazy eight count down (Annie won), Jenga, & many other fun games.

A highlight was sprinting to Lake Superior from the sauna last night & jumping in!! The air was about 50 degrees, & the water colder! We called it the "Inaugi Boggy" and hopefully there will be more to come . . . each year.

Claire, June 1, 2008

I am not going to write that much b/c I just finished writing 37 notes for the CC team b/c our banquet is tomorrow. It's weird that I'm already a senior. I had to write my senior speech today and I remember Claire reading hers 6 years ago. It's been a pretty good senior year so far. I was accepted to Michigan and our team was 4th at states (I was all-state 21st).

It's been a pretty great stay so far and it was really nice that Emma could come. But I miss Annie and Claire coming up and playing big family card games like we used to. . . .

We took a walk like usual to the big lake and that was fun, but we have to head home tomorrow and pick up Bubbie b/c she is coming to my banquet. Papa passed away not long ago and that has been pretty hard because we all know he was a pretty special guy (with the best smile ever). But he is in our thoughts, and hopefully Bubbie will move in with us soon. Claire's in Eugene, Annie's still at State, although applying to grad school. Mommy and Daddy are taking a sauna right now and Jac is sitting on his bed looking cute, as always. I hope to return soon!

Julia, November 14, 2009

Laura writes in the journal religiously. She tends to describe some of our camp activities, but also reflects on family. The first decade or so our girls were mostly with us. Now their visits are more infrequent, and the journal helps to summarize their goings on.

Bob, Jac and I had a wonderful wintery spring break getaway. This is our first ski-in without any children. Claire finishes up her last term at U of M and graduates the end of this month, Annie is a sophomore at MSU and Julia is on a kayaking trip to Mexico with the Bruder's. We joked that with the heavy, blizzardy conditions of yesterday, it is like we are at the opposite ends of the earth from Julia.

We began spring break with a one-night stay at the Ojibwe Hotel in downtown Sault Ste. Marie and had a yummy Mexican meal at the bar next door. We left early in the morning and had a leisurely ski into Boggy's, digging out the camp at about noon. We can't seem to make it in in much less than two hours, even though we didn't haul much in, weren't slowed by young children and Jac trotted along at a steady pace. I hate to think we are just getting slow.

The weather prediction held true. We went to bed to lightly falling snow and woke up to a different world with everything covered in a white blanket of fresh snow. It weighed heavy on the branches, making them lean over and touch the ground, some snapping with the weight. One jack pine fell where we normally park our car. Luckily no car there this trip. We hiked with snowshoes in the morning, trudging through deep drifts with the snow and wind still blowing. The usual trails all looked so different . . . We did frighten a coyote who for some reason didn't catch wind of us. The snow was so deep, he had trouble running away from us and we all had a good clear eye-to-eye look at each other.

Today was like a different place, with blue skies and temperatures into the 40s. We skied over to the Big Lake with Jac and played on the mountains of ice that extended into the lake.

It was an incredibly relaxing trip with the usual naps, sauna, cribbage, reading and food. I really felt I needed this time as life has been busy with get-ting used to subbing in 4th grade.

I look forward to coming back soon, perhaps in early May with all of the girls and Bob to Celebrate Annie's birthday.

Laura, April 2, 2008

Two Hearted River at Boggy's Camp, April 2, 2008.

Wonderful to be here and enjoy Boggy's with dear friends (Mary and BJ) and family (Karner clan). Just returned from a very special 3-week trip to Seattle! I got to spend Q time with Annie, Maxim and Dima. And Julia returned to Seattle from her Spain/Israel trip in time to start PT school. We heard about her travels and Julia planted some seeds, perhaps Bob and I will walk the Camino. She inspired us. Looking forward to December when the Seattle family is planning to come for a bit, can't wait.

Laura, October 13, 2019

A special Boggy's visit with all of our family, except Julia who we are thinking of and miss very much. Julia is in Seattle, just finished first year of PT school and plans to be home for a visit in about 10 days.

We left TC in two car loads; the Karner family in one, and the Otwell, Otwell-Kostylev crew in the other. This was Dima's first visit to Boggy's, we left the day after his 1st birthday celebration. Annie and Maxim are visiting for an extended period (arrived August 18 and will fly back Sept. 12). They plan to visit Maxim's parents in South Bend.

Laura, August 21–25, 2020

Here is a short post by me, perhaps a prelude to my working on this book.

We have returned to Boggy's after 4 days at Lake Superior Provincial Park. We camped on an island in Lake Mijinemungshing that we camped at w/ Thompsons in 1998. Laura, Julia, Jac and I had a nice trip, many loons, nice weather.

I have wondered and contemplated the beauty of the Two Hearted River valley. The beauty is multi-dimensional and ever changing:

Open space (height, width, length)
River (level, velocity, frozen, fish, sand, gravel, logs)
Weather (rain, wind, snow, sun, fog)
Flora (seasonal, flowers, riverbank, trees)
Fauna (birds, bugs, fishermen, mammals, Otwells, canoers)

Bob, August 19, 2005

It has been a pleasure to share Boggy's Camp with family and friends. My Dad organized yearly family fishing trips. Normally the trips centered around fishing for trout in the spring, in Canada. In the 1970s through the early 1990s, he flew his float plane up to a small lake and we would stay nearby at a lodge on the Little White River in Ontario. Other family members would drive up, and we would fish some of the small lakes in the area. My Dad would fly back to the lakes, and the rest of us would huff up the hills, carrying canoes. In 1995 and 1996 my Dad was in his early 80s, and his flying days were nearing an end. We missed the spring trip, so we did Boggy's fishing and hunting trips.

Boggy Deer Camp
Skip, Brian & John, John, Mark & Mike, Dad, Bob and Annie
   Otwells drove almost 7 hours in pouring rain—clouds hid lunar eclipse. Bob's good directions helped us find our way on a stormy night. Good food all weekend but fishing was poor, and hunting was worse. However, all shooters were successful at clay pigeon range. John Woods arrived in brand new Dodge Dakota truck—Snappy. Many folks snoring in bunkroom—everyone blaming everyone else.
   Everyone had a nice visit, hope to return soon.

Skip Otwell

Nice color on river valley. Bob seeded riverbank and stabilized same with felled trees cabled to bank. Township Park filled. Nice trip to Rainbow Lodge and outlet of Two Hearted River.

Bill Otwell, September 29, 1996

We have had many friends join us at Boggy's. I can easily say that the friend who loves Boggy's Camp the most is Tim Scott. Tim grew up in the small southern Michigan farm town of Millington. He studied Civil Engineering at Michigan Tech University in Houghton. After graduation he moved to Traverse City to work with us at Otwell Mawby P.C. The first autumn we owned Boggy's we invited OMPC staff up for an October retreat. Tim, my partner Roger Mawby, and two dogs joined me, and we travelled north for some hunting, cycling, cutting wood and good eats. We also had OMPC retreats for several more years. Eventually we started to get greater participation from all staff. Activities also evolved to include kickball, euchre, and poker.

Boggy's fishing camp 1995: Mark, Dad, Stan, Rob, me, John, and in front Claire and Annie.

Otwell Mawby staff retreat 1993: Dan, Tim, Laura, Jerry, Lori, Roger, Mike, and Sue.

Tim was at all these gatherings, along with dinners at Boggy's with our family and friends. Tim is family.

In those early years, Tim was a bachelor and flexible with his time. Following are excerpts from a few of Tim's entries, including his honeymoon, and then with the addition of his children.

Solo trip to Boggy's. It is so good to be back here; I didn't realize how much I've missed this place. I came here to retreat from the everyday race of life and have some extended time with the Lord. There's no better place than Boggy's for that . . .

Tim Scott, June 6, 1999

The honeymooners arrived Monday evening after a shortened stay at Drummond Island. The call to Boggy's was too strong. Nothing compares to Boggy's. After being married on May 6 we headed to Drummond Island for some hiking, biking and canoeing, but after about one day we decided to head for Boggy's. We stopped at Tahquamenon Falls on the way and had a great meal at the Camp 33 brew pub. On Tuesday, we went to Grand Marais and the log slide (what a view), also hiked Sable Dunes. On the way back we went to Pretty Lake and portaged through 4 lakes. Wednesday and Thursday, we spent at Boggy's, kicking back, R & R. Had a nice hike to lake and did some fishing. A lot of fish in the river (none in frying pan). A few fishermen around. I met and talked to Jim McCarley, former Boggy's owner, he's a good fisherman, and nice guy.

I also talked to the guy who witnessed a big hawk fly into the window by the fridge last year. He said it was quite a sight & sound. The hawk shook it off and flew away. No broken windows yet this year.

We had an awesome time at Boggy's, there's no other place we'd rather have been. Thanks a lot. The Newly Weds.

Tim & Monica, May 8–11, 2000

Price tag on Boggy's Journal notebook $1.99; the entries in it and the memories created here, priceless. Just finished our 4th day in a row of hiking to lakeshore. Originally, on our way up we talked about going over to Pictured Rocks Lakeshore for a day. But once at Boggy's Camp, we have no desire to drive anywhere. Besides, one hike to the lakeshore from Boggy's and you realize *there is a pictured rocks lakeshore right here. Amazingly beautiful. I challenged the kids to find two rocks alike. They couldn't do it . . .*

Tim and Monica, Meghan, Jonathon, Claire, Thomas, Charles, Maxwell and Jane, August 23, 2018

Tim's and Monica's were not the only Boggy's honeymoon. Our Claire had a friend who honeymooned at Boggy's in October 2012, and Claire and Jesse did so the previous summer. In addition, Annie and Maxim got married at the Grand Traverse County courthouse in July 2016, and then we all went to Boggy's. Annie and Maxim were travelling west to Seattle to their new home. Not a classic honeymoon for two, but with all the Otwells, and of course, the Scott family was also there.

Jesse & I came up to Boggy's for 4 days for our honeymoon! Super relaxing after a fun/stressful/overwhelming week leading up to our wedding. We were married at the Leelanau School 8/18 and lucked out w/perfect weather & it was such a great celebration with all of our closest family and friends. I have been looking forward to bringing Jesse to Boggy's for quite some time, but living in Oregon makes it difficult for us to get up here. We arrived to a beautiful sign that read "Welcome Newlyweds—Boggy's Honeymoon Haven!" with Champagne, Junior Mints, truffles, candles & white ribbon! So NICE! Thanks family.

We tried to fit as many activities into our short week as possible. Hiked to Lake Superior for a swim, canoed up the Two Hearted to Reed & Green Bridge, Jesse and I went jogging, got two bikes out one day, took a sauna, had a bonfire, spent an afternoon at Perch Lake, and relaxed as much as possible. I taught Jesse how to play cribbage. We also drove to Rainbow Lodge to take a look at some of the damage from the forest fire. We wanted to canoe to the mouth but forgot the racks for the car.

This has been a wonderful week w/my new husband!! We need to move back here so we can come up here more than once every 3 years.

Claire, 8/20/12–8/23/12

We had a wonderful trip time at Boggy's! I was so happy to be able to make a trip after 6 years . . . way too long! I hope we will be back here much sooner. It was also Maxim's first trip here which was wonderful. I have wanted him to experience Boggy's for a long time. It was also wonderful to be up here with my sisters and parents all together, and the Scott family joined us. The blueberries were great, Lake Superior was perfect, and we went on nice walks and ate good food—a great time at Boggy's. . . .

Annie, 7/30/16 to 8/2/16

CHAPTER 18

FRED "BOGGY" YOUNG

So, who was Boggy? Boggy will always be part of our U.P. experience. When we sit down for a meal at our camp, we often propose a toast, *"Thank You Boggy."*

As already described in some newspaper clippings, Boggy had friends and family who enjoyed going up to Boggy's Camp for fishing or hunting, starting as early as the 1930s. We are not sure when the camp was built, but my best guess is that it was in the late 1930s. The story we heard is that Boggy hired a carpenter to build the cabin. The carpenter built it on the wrong bend in the river, not on land Boggy owned. The cabin was constructed on state land.

We have a deed that reflects a 1944 land exchange between the State of Michigan and Fred Young. Boggy got the two acres we own with a little over 300 feet of river frontage. The state received 20 acres that Boggy owned, but not on the river. The 1944 exchange had language that preserved public access to the river, and the right for the state to make stream bank improvements.

The "carpenter built it on the wrong bend of river" story never rang true to me. Boggy did not own property on the river. I have also wondered if Boggy would have gotten someone else to build the camp. I think he, and his family and friends, would have built the cabin. That is the way in the U.P., and perhaps the normal way everywhere in the depression years of the 1930s.

Brothers-in-law Harold and Sherwin Overholt bought Boggy's Camp in 1948 for $1, and their family owned it from 1948–1981. Jim and Judy McCarley bought Boggy's in 1981 and owned it from 1981–1991. Their family spent much of each summer there. The McCarleys built the sauna; the other buildings look like they predated 1981.

Here is Boggy's obituary, published in the November 6, 1958, edition of the *Newberry News*.

Fred Young Passes
Fred Young, one of Newberry's most widely known citizens, died in a Marquette hospital Monday afternoon after being hospitalised for this past six weeks.

He was born in Southport, England on April 15, 1885 and came to Newberry with his parents, the late Mr. and Mrs. Harry Young, in 1895, and had resided here since.

"Boggy" was a member of one of the early graduating classes of the Newberry schools, and for a time was employed by D.H.S. and A. railroad. He worked for a time at the Charcoal Iron Co. as an engineer and was in charge of machine shop operations at the local plant. For about twenty years he was undersheriff of Luce county, and attendance officer for the Newberry schools, retiring two years ago.

He was a veteran of World War I, a member of the American legion, and McMillan Lodge No. 400, F: & A.M., and was senior warden of All Saints Episcopal church in Newberry.

"Boggy," as he was affectionately known by thousands, was more than a senior citizen in this community. He was almost an institution. With an abiding concern for the less fortunate in life, he was prominent in Goodfellow and other charitable work and always willing to lend a hand. In his work as attendance officer he knew every youngster for miles around, hazed them to school, bought them clothing and supplies when he couldn't bulldoze some merchant into doing it, and was a staunch defender of the kids in their troubles. Truly, his memory will endure kindly in the minds of all who knew him.

Surviving him are a son Russel, of Denver, Colo; one brother, Roy, of Newberry; four sisters, Florence and Rena Young of Newberry, Mrs. S. M. (Mae)

*Overholt and Mrs. Harold C. (Dessalee) Overholt of Marquette; a niece Jan
Powers of Ashlee; a nephew, Don Young of Jackson; and two grand nieces.*

*Funeral services were held Wednesday afternoon at All Saints Episcopal
Church, Fr. Wm. Wiedrich officiating. Burial was in Forest Home Cemetery.*

The Mackinac Bridge opened almost exactly one year before Boggy's death.
Yoopers call those of us who live below (south) of the bridge "trolls." I
wonder if Boggy ever imagined his beloved U.P. filling up with trolls, as the
bridge made access so much easier?

We have learned a little about his life in addition to the information
in the obituary. According to the 1900 census, 15-year-old Boggy was living at home in Newberry with his mother and father, Adelade and Harry,
along with Florence (18), Roy (11), Harold (6), Mae (4) and Rena (1). His
brother Harold died in 1902. In 1910, Boggy was living in a rental house in
Sault Ste. Marie with his wife, Ann, and a newborn son, Russel.

By 1920, Boggy was back living in Newberry, was single and working as a machinist. He was living with his parents and two sisters. His son,
Russel, was living with Eveline and Marshal Smith, an aunt and uncle. I
could not trace the whereabouts of
his former wife, Ann.

According to Sterling McGinn
with the *Newberry News*, the
Youngs were well known in Newberry, owning a big white house on
Harrie Street, right across from the
courthouse. Boggy played baseball,
and his brother Roy was an excellent player, earning the nickname
"Cy" after the famous professional
pitcher Cy Young from the turn of
the century.

Boggy (standing) and his brother
Roy "Cy" Young, 1908 Newberry
baseball team. *Source: Sterling
McGinn Photograph Collection*

Roy was a custodian across the street at the courthouse. Boggy's sisters Mae and Dessalee married two Overholt brothers and moved to Marquette. The older sisters, Rena (who worked at the railroad) and Florence, never married and stayed in the family home.

From census records, Boggy's parents purchased the home on Harrie Street and were living there in 1930, with Boggy and his two sisters. Boggy was still a machinist at the local chemical plant. By 1940, his parents had passed away, and Boggy was still in the house with his two older sisters. By that time, he was working as a school truant officer. In the 1950 census, Boggy was in the same position, and living with his two sisters.

Former home of Young family on Harrie Street in Newberry, Michigan, 2023.

Three lodgers also lived in the house in 1950, one of them being Leland Anderson. Interestingly, Leland (Andy) Anderson was the head of the Fisheries Division of the MDNR in Newberry. He wrote the already referred to *Two Hearted River: Leland Anderson* in 1973 and had worked for the MDNR since the 1940s. Is it a coincidence that Boggy received a piece of land from the state in 1944 that just happens to be on a great stretch of that river for trout fishing? So much coincidence here, I need to try to fill in the blanks.

The View from Boggy's Camp, spring 1939

Boggy Young, his brother-in-law Sherwin Overholt, future brother-in-law Harold Overholt and a few other friends were fishing on the Two Hearted River. There was no structure, just a canvas tent. Inside were a cook stove, tables, cots and plenty of food and liquor. Their tent was located on state land, and they had set it up in the same place overlooking the river for spring fishing, and fall deer hunting, for the last few years.

Leland (Andy) Anderson, a 26-year-old Chicago native and a recent forestry graduate from U of M, stopped by to fish. He loved the U.P. and had recently moved to Newberry. Andy had been coming up to the Two Hearted to fish whenever his schedule allowed. He was a bachelor.

John Saxton was also fishing there that weekend. (John was still fishing that stretch of the Two Hearted when we met him in the early 1990s.)

The men all agreed that the fishing on the gravel beds at that location on the river was wonderful. This was the best place on the main branch to fish. They brought out the good scotch to celebrate the morning of fishing. And to discuss some plans.

The discussion evolved to building a small cabin on the river, right where their tent was. But it was state land. Boggy owned 20 acres of land, nearby, not on the river. Boggy offered, "well, we could ask permission, or we could just build the cabin, and then ask forgiveness." They built the cabin and called it Boggy's Camp.

Well, that could have been how it happened. The cabin was built, I think in the late 1930s, and Boggy did a land exchange with the state in 1944 to secure the land he had already built the cabin on.

One family connection we have with Boggy is that my mom's parents, sister, and brother (the Garsides) also immigrated from Southport, England, around the turn of the last century. They moved to Barrie, Ontario, where my mom was born in 1914. Southport had a population of about 50,000 people in 1900. I wonder if the Southport Garsides knew the Southport Youngs. Why do you leave England and move to the North American wilderness? Another story.

With all the conversations I have recently had, I have been unable to track down someone that actually met Boggy. I never asked John Saxton, the fisherman we met 30 years ago, but he probably knew Boggy. We put an ad in the Newberry paper in January 2023 that ran for a few weeks, to no avail.

In August 2023, we visited his grave at Forest Home cemetery in Newberry. The cemetery is located a mile from the former family home. Boggy, his parents, one brother, and three sisters are all buried together with a simple flat gravestone for each. There is also a large monument with "YOUNG" written on it. His younger sister Dessalee Overholt was buried in the family plot, along with her husband Harold. She died in 1994, a few years after we had purchased Boggy's. I could have (should have) met her and learned more about her big brother.

There was a flag commemorating military service next to Harold's marker. The other grave markers looked to be unattended to for many years. Newberry seems to have forgotten Boggy and his family.

CHAPTER 19

LAST THOUGHTS

The View from Boggy's Camp, 2050

The river is running clean, clear, cold, and dark. The forest is maturing, the diversity of the flora and fauna increasing, the trees are soaring. The oldest pines have fallen, leaving gaps of sunlight on the forest floor where young trees compete. Beavers are plentiful, their many dams helping to expand the wetlands and preventing the carbon rich peat from drying out.

Dawson Creek, named for a former logging camp owner, has been renamed to honor the Ojibwe. The Two Hearted River has been elevated to personhood status.

At Boggy's, the propane tank is gone. Solar panels provide electricity for lights, stove, and refrigerator. The hand water pump along with the wood stoves used for cabin heat and the sauna are still in place. Some things must stay the same.

There is an electric vehicle charging station at Pine Stump. Electric bikes and cars pass the camp, slowly and quietly. More people walk by, as hiking continues to increase in popularity, and hiking trails expand.

The fifth generation of Otwells are enjoying Boggy's Camp and the beauty of this little watershed on the south shore of Lake Superior. I have moved on.

The View from Boggy's Camp, 2050 is the optimist's view. An alternate, dystopian view is also possible. I am not a pessimist. I hope our society is smart enough to slow climate change, and limit bad outcomes.

I appreciate our time at Boggy's Camp and in the surrounding forests even more after reviewing our journals and learning more about the watershed drafting this book. The river seems protected. The Natural River program controls development in many ways and strives to reduce human-induced impacts to the river. An extra layer of protection may evolve as we look to maintain our natural resources in ways initially practiced by Indigenous people.

Indigenous tribes have promoted a novel way to protect rivers, by giving them personhood status. In Brazil, 2023, the local community passed a law, proposed by an Indigenous council member, that designates the Komi Memem River and its tributaries as living entities with rights. These rights include maintaining the natural flow, and protection of the surrounding forests that make up the watershed. Laws with these protections have also been written in New Zealand and Chile. In the US, in 2018, a local Ojibwe tribe sued the State of Minnesota on behalf of manoomin (wild rice). The tribe argued that manoomin had a legal right to grow and be preserved. In 2019, citizens of Toledo, Ohio, granted personhood rights to Lake Erie.

If the Two Hearted was a person, what would she be like? Most of all she would be steady. Whenever we visit, she is flowing steadily, water coming around the bend upstream of Boggy's Camp and disappearing around the next one downstream. Her mood changes based on weather and flora. She is normally shallow and dark, her color and reflections varying with the sun and time of day. She is flanked by color depending on the location and season: tan from exposed sand banks; green from many evergreens, along with maples, dogwood and alders in the summer; red, orange, and yellow maple leaves in autumn and red dogwood branches that pop out when the leaves are absent. She is often flanked by snow from November to May. Sometimes she is completely hidden under snow and ice, falsely presenting herself as a wide, safe white trail through the forest. But then as one travels around a bend, a visible dark shadow in the ice will be seen and you are reminded to be aware; she is there, flowing steady.

She does get angry, sometimes violent, each spring. She is filled with water from the snowpack, and rises four to six feet, sometimes more. Instead of placidly floating canoes and kayaks as she does in the summer, she erodes the sand banks and rips out trees. She churns and boils, and rushes everything she touches downstream. In a few weeks, she will be back to her normal, peaceful self. The Two Hearted has been behaving this way for thousands of years, after she first cut her path through the glacial till.

The ownership of the land in the watershed has changed many times over the past 200 years, when no one owned the land, and the Indigenous people occupied and were stewards of it. Once the government surveyed and platted the land, they sold it to private logging companies. These companies cut down and abused the forest and the river with one goal—maximize board-feet of lumber. Now most of the watershed is owned by the State of Michigan, the Nature Conservancy, and private forest reserves. Professional foresters plan and monitor forest management activities. These recent changes are positive. The 200-year-old white pines near Boggy's started growing before anyone owned this land. These old pines have survived all these property ownership changes, and they will die a natural death.

What happened to the threat from the former major property owner in the watershed, Benson Forests? According to a November 25, 1994, *Detroit Free Press* article, Ben Benson had a heart attack in 1993 and was hospitalized. In 1994, he sold his home in Marquette and sold his share of Benson Forests. These lands included 94,000 acres of former Cleveland-Cliffs property in Luce County. Most of the former Benson lands in the Two Hearted watershed are now owned by the Nature Conservancy or are part of private forest reserves. Writer Dixie Franklin was quoted in a *Free Press* article about Benson: "He just didn't fit into the U.P. Up here it's 10 years before they recognize you as a stranger."

We have appreciated our many interactions with Yoopers over the past decades. We only own two acres, so we have purchased all the firewood for the woodstove from locals. With no cell service, all communication must happen before we get to the camp. The locals always show up and deliver what we agreed upon, or more. We have interacted with propane delivery and septic tank pump-out men, and a contractor who built a new metal roof for our camp. The work is always top notch, even though sometimes fishing will delay the schedule. Sharing a beer at our camp normally seals the deal.

Yoopers are strong, independent folks who love their freedom. The

U.P. contains 27% of Michigan's land area, but only 3% of the population. Room to roam. They have their own dialect, influenced by early settlers to the region. When Michigan's successful marketing campaign was launched in the 1980s, *"Say Yes to Michigan,"* a U.P. phrase was quickly born, *"Say ya to da U.P., eh?"*

Laura and I feel so lucky to have grown up and live in Michigan. Two beautiful peninsulas surrounded by four of the five Great Lakes. We have done some travelling out of state and are always happy to come home. The four seasons are all enjoyable, each of them awesome in their own way. Even though it comes late to Northern Michigan, spring is a rebirth. Everything greens up so completely. Summer is being outside, outdoor sports, and living with influxes of tourists who come to visit Northern Michigan's lakes, forests, wineries, and pubs. Fall is the most beautiful. Cool, crisp air, the forest lights up with reds and yellows. Then winter, gorgeous with a fresh cover of snow.

Boggy's Camp, with some minor maintenance of the cabin, seems secure in its future. After 30+ years of battle on the bank, the river won. I am OK with that. When we canoe downstream, many other south-facing high

Laura and Bob, outside Boggy's Camp, August 2023.

banks are mostly bare sand, even those remote banks that see little traffic from people fishing. The bank in front of the cabin is still well protected with large trees and vegetation. Boggy's Camp, protected by Boggy's ghost and set high above the Two Hearted River, will continue looking down on the river for many years. Laura and I hope to be there for a few more of them.

We are firmly into the fourth generation of Otwells enjoying Boggy's. Since we purchased the camp in 1991, Laura and I added one to our brood, our parents have passed on, and we have added two sons-in-law and four grandkids. Claire and Jesse live in Traverse City with Blaise and Sarai. Claire is a township planner. Julia also lives in Traverse City and is a physical therapist in private practice. Annie and Maxim live in Washington, DC, with Dima and Amira. Annie is a microbiologist and works for the government. In the summer of 2023, Annie wrote some recollections of our trips to Boggy's when she and her sisters were young.

> *"It's too dark! It's too dark!" I yelled while trying to go to sleep in the pitch-black bunkroom at Boggy's. I don't actually remember yelling this, and I'm not sure if I yelled it on one occasion or multiple. I do know that this phrase, like many others, became a phrase of our childhood. A phrase that our family would make jokes about and that our family alone knew the meaning of. A phrase that evoked images of the Boggy's experience that we all shared. The blackness of the night with no streetlights outside or light switches inside. Three little girls in their sleeping bags sleeping on the squeaky old mattresses on the bottom bunks. My bunk to the left of the hallway door—the bunk that always seemed to have the most evidence of mouse activity when we arrived. A little scared of the pitch blackness of the night and the mouse sounds but mostly enjoying the Boggy's experience. When I think back on my childhood, memories like these with my family at Boggy's are sprinkled throughout. Time spent together at Boggy's and the memories we share are part of the glue that binds our family together.*
>
> *Many of these memories are made up of activities we did year after year at Boggy's—what became part of the typical Boggy's routine. After highlights like crossing the Mackinac Bridge and shopping for groceries in Newberry (the bulk candy section was our favorite!), we would guess how many campers were at Reed and Green campground—always a competition but I'm not sure if there*

was ever a prize. When we were little and we still had the Suburban (surpris-
ing now I know for my sustainability-minded parents), we were allowed to
unbuckle our seatbelts and sit in the Way Back to go over The Bumps. The last
stretch of dirt road between the campground and our cabin was particularly
bumpy and my dad (who was usually driving those days) would power over
those bumps, with us three girls bouncing around and laughing in the Way
Back of the Burb. One year we came, and The Bumps were suddenly much less
(the County had probably graded the road). We were sad about it. I remember
going out to the road by myself to secretly try to recreate The Bumps, which I
assumed my whole family would be grateful for. As I sat in the road making
piles of sand, my dad walked by and explained how The Bumps were actually
holes in the road. I felt silly.

Summertime meant blueberry picking and blueberry pancake breakfasts.
Walks on the sandy roads to Lake Superior. Canoeing and swimming in the
Two Hearted. Too many biting insects—mosquitoes or black flies or deer flies
and horse flies, depending on the exact time of summer. Wintertime meant
skiing in the last 5 miles of roads that didn't get plowed. We would wear back-
packs and our dad would pull a sled. One year there was so much snow that
our dad shoveled off the roof of the cabin and we slid off the roof! One year was
so warm that we skied in T-shirts and had competitions at Lake Superior for
how long we could stand in the frigid waters. Any time of the year meant fam-
ily meals together, reading, relaxing, and card games . . . so many card games!
Our family has always loved to play cards together (cribbage, hearts, spades,
pinochle, pounce . . .) and Boggy's has always offered a perfect setting to do so.

Many Boggy's memories are with my sisters, as we enjoyed the freedom to
explore the natural surroundings without much else to do besides play. Across
multiple years and Boggy's trips, we constructed Boggy's Funland. Scattered
throughout the forest, we made a swing, a teeter totter, and a wooden fort with
a painted sign. The fall that we made the teeter totter, the yellowjackets seemed
to be especially abundant and you could hear the woods buzzing. We needed
a large log for the teeter totter, but we were worried to trample through the
forest and come across a hive in the ground. We suited up from head to toe in
protective clothing (including mosquito head nets) and ventured out into the
woods. We found the perfect log and avoided any stings.

Other deeply ingrained Boggy's memories are sensory reminders of the place:
the dry lichen crunching under our feet as we hiked through the forest, the

fresh scent of pine needles baking in the sun on the sandy trails, the sound of the waves crashing as we approached Lake Superior, the smell of the sauna, the feeling of swimming in the cold, dark, earthy water of the Two Hearted. Boggy's is truly a special place. Since graduating college in 2010, I have lived in New York, California, Washington, and now Washington, DC. Combined with two young kids, it has been hard to get up to Boggy's as often as I would like lately. I hope this will change soon as we are hoping to move back to Michigan in the near future. I hope my kids can grow up experiencing the sights, sounds, smells, and overall feeling of Boggy's.

"Let's move to Boggy's!" was another family phrase of my childhood. Mainly our parents would say it in a lighthearted way—somewhat of a joke. I think this phrase also represented a yearning for the simpler, more pure life that Boggy's offered us. Away from work, school, sports, technology, politics, certain daily responsibilities, and distractions. A time that our family could just be together. A type of escape—a sanctuary—that most people do not have access to. During my most recent trip to Boggy's I went on a run with my husband, and we stopped by Lake Superior to dip and gaze—no other people in sight. It is incredible how majestic, vast, and untouched it felt. This natural, wild beauty felt in such a dichotomy with the scary things of the present day—worsening climate change and dire climate predictions, a global pandemic . . . all that I could do at that moment was take it in and feel grateful. I will always feel grateful for our family times together at Boggy's—enjoying the natural beauty and peace of the forest, Lake Superior, and the Two Hearted River.

I cannot reflect on our family's past adventures at Boggy's, or the future of the watershed (and the world it is in), without thinking about climate change. Our society is continually learning new ways climate change will affect both the built environment and the natural world. One known effect of climate change is larger rainstorms and subsequent flooding due to increased moisture in the air. Increased droughts are a second. The unfortunate synergy between these two events is that drought reduces plant growth and can harden surface soils. Droughts also can be a precursor to forest fires. These phenomena can then increase flood peaks because there is less vegetation to slow the large flood flows, and less plant absorption of the precipitation. Fire and water!

Across North America, wildfires, smoke, massive storms, and rare weather events are increasing in frequency and affecting more regions. In the winter of 2023 and 2024, California was slammed by one atmospheric river after another. Rainfall totals over a few weeks surpassed annual average totals. In Traverse City, the winter of 2024 was the worst in my memory. There was no snow. We cross-country skied once in November, the snow melted, and then we had a nice snowstorm in mid-January where we skied and snowshoed. That snow was gone by the end of the month, and that is not what we are used to in "Snow Country." The weather is weird.

The Two Hearted watershed will be more resilient to large rain events than many other watersheds. Spring rains in combination with snow melt normally gorge the watershed every spring. The basin will be better prepared to absorb unprecedented rain events from a summer or fall deluge. If the low snow years continue, that will affect animal behavior, and can close businesses that depend on snow.

Practicing hydrology these days is challenging. The climate statistics on which the profession relies are in flux. When I studied engineering and began my career in the 1970s and 1980s, the 100 years of rainfall records were deemed solid to predict frequency. Now, scientists do not even consider these older rainfall records. The data do not pertain to today's climate. The 100-year flood mapping I did in Southern California in the late 1970s is now worthless.

Our society currently gives lip service to climate change. The State of Michigan and the U.S. Government are pledging substantial changes over the next decades. Worldwide, many countries are more vulnerable and are ahead of the U.S. in their policies and practice. There are many possibilities to reduce our greenhouse gas emissions. We know the problem, and we know how to fix it.

Many of the changes to reduce our impact on the planet require citizen cooperation. Most of us in the U.S. enjoy our pampered life and niceties, and we will not give them up easily. Air conditioning, large SUVs, wide roads sprawling outward from city centers, and warm homes filled with stuff ordered through Amazon are part of our status quo. Does reducing greenhouse gas emissions require more political will, or the will of the people?

Even with persistent drought and forest fires in the Southwest, that area continues to grow. Michigan is mentioned as a location for climate refuge, yet our population continues to dwindle. Even with more efficient use of our limited resources, and a hopeful slowing of the growth rate of greenhouse gas emissions, we are entering a phase of adaptation.

Forestry management continues to evolve. Historically, forest management has focused on increasing wood resources, not maximizing carbon capture or other forest benefits. In the Two Hearted watershed, the State of Michigan, the Nature Conservancy, and the forest reserves are practicing sustainable and resilient forestry practices. Wood resources are still needed for paper, cardboard, and lumber. Mass timber is a new construction method, at least for the U.S., which uses structural wood products to construct large commercial buildings. The use of wood instead of steel and concrete has a lower carbon footprint. This can help mitigate climate change and utilize Two Hearted watershed wood products. The MDNR is now building an office building in Newberry with these techniques.

More research is coming to light regarding the complexity of forests and their critical value beyond just lumber. Trees and many other plants are interconnected and communicate through their roots and beneficial fungi. As the forest ages, the capacity to grab carbon increases. A recent book by Ben Rawlence, *The Treeline,* drives home this concept.

> *The northern trees interest Diana because they have evolved in the harshest conditions. They have learned lessons, contain hormones and have survived strategies that other plants will need to learn with climate change. And they contain chemicals that are essential for humans, if only science could find the time and resources to pay proper attention. Then, she says, perhaps we would think differently about how we harvest trees—timber may in fact be the least valuable use for the forest.*

The Diana to whom he refers is Diana Beresford-Kroeger, a distinguished scientist who has done remarkable research, not at a university, but on her own property in Ontario. This research and other growing knowledge will help us live more naturally and adapt more easily to change. The evolving forestry practices in the Two Hearted watershed will not halt climate change. However, having this real laboratory with rivers, forests, and wetlands will help us learn more about our environment. We will appreciate our wildlands as a future haven for wildlife and as a tangible benefit for humans. These untouched lands can be part of a solution for better stewardship of the earth.

My favorite place in the world to sit is on the old wood bench near Boggy's west property line. The bench overlooks the Two Hearted River. There are good views downstream to the east, down a long stretch of fast-flowing riffled water, and views upstream of the slow-winding river. When gusty wind blows, one can observe the water surface shiver. When the wind is calm, and during summer low flows, one can hear the river tumble over the gravel beds. The river is dark, but the sunlight can bring out silver and grey highlights, along with red reflections from the dogwood. In the quiet backwaters beneath the bench, we have observed salmon making depressions in the gravel to spawn.

The setting is normally quiet, often interrupted by a red squirrel chattering, letting us know that we are in their territory. If our dog Marta is with me, my consciousness is raised because she is intently taking nature in through her eyes, ears, and nose. The squirrels are more irritated with Marta present.

Often Laura is with me on the bench, and we talk about life: our family, our camp, our home and friends, our plans. This past summer we celebrated our 40th wedding anniversary. They say a long marriage is simply a long conversation. Our long conversation has been full of life. Boggy's Camp has helped put it in perspective.

BIBLIOGRAPHY

Authors

Anderson, Leland, *Two Hearted River: Leland Anderson,* Michigan Dept. of Natural Resources, Fisheries Division, October 1973.

Baker, Carlos, *Ernest Hemingway: A Life Story,* Charles Scribner's Sons, New York, 1969.

Baker, Sheridan, *Hemingway's Two Hearted River. Michigan Alumnus Quarterly,* February 28, 1959.

Beal, James William, *Lessons on Growing Forest Trees,* Issue 21 of Bulletin, Experiment Station, Agricultural College of Michigan, 1886.

Beresford-Kroeger, Diana, *To Speak for the Trees: My Life's Journey from Ancient Celtic Wisdom to a Healing Vision of the Forest,* Random House Canada, 2019.

Bergquist, S.G., *The Glacial History and Development of Michigan.*

Cleland, Charles E., *The Place of the Pike (Gnoozhekaaning): A History of the Bay Mills Indian Community,* University of Michigan Press, 2001.

Dennis, Jerry and Date, Craig, *Canoeing Michigan Rivers*, Friede Publications, Davison, Michigan, 1986.

Elliott, Gerald, *Hemingway's Wrong River*, undated news clipping.

Fongers, Dave, *Two Hearted River Watershed Hydrologic Study*, Hydrologic Studies Unit Land and Water Management Division, Michigan Department of Environmental Quality, January 18, 2007.

Franklin, Dixie, *Con Culhane, Lumberman's legends still rival Paul Bunyan's image*, Upbeat article, dated June 25, 1978. Article displayed at Tahquamenon Logging Museum, Newberry, Michigan, 2022.

Franz, Dale Clark, *Pigeon River Country: A Michigan Forest*, University of Michigan Press, 2007.

Hall, Dennis. A July 1975 version of the saying appeared as part of an article titled "The Land Is Borrowed from Our Children" by Dennis J. Hall that was published in the periodical "Michigan Natural Resources." Hall worked at the Office of Land Use for the State of Michigan. Others have also been credited with this saying.

Hemingway, Ernest, *The Complete Short Stories of Ernest Hemingway*, Scribner Book Company, New York, 1987.

Henderson, F.M., *Open Channel Flow*, Macmillan, 1966.

Hinsdale, Wilbert B., *Archaeological atlas of Michigan*, University of Michigan, 2008, originally printed 1931. https://quod.lib.umich.edu/g/genpub/1265156.0001.001/1.

Karamanski, Theodore, *Deep Woods Frontier: A History of Logging in Northern Michigan*, Wayne State University Press, Detroit, 1989.

Longtine, Sonny, *Michigan's Upper Peninsula: Life, legends & landmarks*, Sunnyside Publications, Marquette, 2002.

McDonnell, Michael A., *Masters of Empire: Great Lakes Indians and the Making of America*, Hill and Wang, 2016.

Moore, Mike, *A Short History of the Michigan State Forests: The Early Days*, 2014, and *A Short History of Early Forestry Education in Michigan*, Michigan State University Extension.

Philip, Leila, *Beaverland: How One Weird Rodent Made America*, Published by Twelve, 2022.

Potter, Agnes, *Agnes Potter Diary of Spile Dam Club*.

Rawlence, Ben, *The Treeline: The Last Forest and the Future of Life on Earth*, St. Martin's Press, 2022.

Reynolds, Terry S. and Dawson, Virginia P., *Iron Will: Cleveland-Cliffs and the Mining of Iron Ore, 1847-2006,* Wayne State University Press, 2011.

Simard, Suzanne, *Finding the Mother Tree: Discovering the Wisdom of the Forest*, Knopf, New York, 2021.

Sitar, Kristie and Roell, Brian, *Factors Limiting Deer Abundance in the Upper Peninsula*, MDNR, 2021.

Spurr, Stephen and Barnes, Burton, *Forest Ecology*, John Wiley and Sons, New York, 1964.

Stonehouse, Frederick, *Lake Superior's Shipwreck Coast*, Avery Color Studios, Au Trail, Michigan, 1985.

Titus, Harold, *The Land Nobody Wanted: The Story of Michigan's Public Domain*, Michigan State College, Agricultural Experiment Station, Special Bulletin 332, April 1945.

Wooster, Margaret, *Meander: Making Room for Rivers*, State University of New York, Albany, 2021.

Organizations

Circle of Blue, *Valuing Nature: White House Publishes Natural Capital Accounting Strategy,* https://www.circleofblue.org/2023/federal-water -tap/federal-water-tap-january-30-valuing-nature-white-house -publishes-natural-capital-accounting-strategy/.

Great Lakes Historical Society, *The Autobiography of Captain Alexander McDougall*, Cleveland, Ohio, 1968.

Michigan Department of Natural Resources, *Eastern Upper Peninsula Regional Forest Management Plan, 2013.*

Michigan Department of Natural Resources, Land and Water Management Division, *Two Hearted River Natural River Plan*, December 1973, updated March 2002.

Michigan Highways, "The Great Routes of the Great Lake State." http://www.michiganhighways.org/history.html.

Michigan State University Extension, *Forest Basics, Michigan Forest History*, https://mff.forest.mtu.edu/PDF/1-TreeBasics/3-History.pdf.

National Park Service: Pictured Rocks: *An Administrative History.* https://www.nps.gov/piro/learn/historyculture/upload/PRNL%20 Administrative%20History.pdf

Northern Michigan University archives, 1915 map of Luce County. https://uparchives.nmu.edu/CCI/Maps/Drawer%206/Folder%20 2/32_6_2_1.jpg.

Superior Watershed Partnership, *Two Hearted River, Watershed Management Plan*, Marquette, May 2008, updated 2020

The Nature Conservancy, *Field Notes from Michigan*, Fall 2022 Newsletter

The Nature Conservancy, *A Good Cut: Restoring the Forests of Michigan's Upper Peninsula*, https://www.nature.org/en-us/get-involved/how-to -help/places-we-protect/two-hearted-river-forest-reserve/

United States Department of Agriculture (USDA) Natural Resources Conservation Service, *Soil Survey of Luce County, Michigan*, 2003

United States Department of the Interior, Fish and Wildlife Service, *National Wetlands Inventory*, 1980.

Acknowledgments

It took an interconnected web of people to put this book together, and I am thankful to all of them. My partner in life, and my confidante in the preparation of this manuscript, is my wife, Laura. She is a thoughtful reader and careful listener. She deftly handles my endless questions and requests, even when her thoughts might be elsewhere. She reminds me of events and details to add to the book because she has lived the Boggy's experience with me. Through the years, Laura has contributed many memorable entries into the Boggy's Camp Journal. She read sections throughout the writing of the document, and read the first draft, providing wise and valued comments.

My three daughters—Claire, Annie, and Julia—made Boggy's a special place for our family with their joy and enthusiasm for a remote place with no running water or electricity. Children always view a place through fresh eyes. The three of them have provided memories and excellent content for the book with their journal entries and 33 years of photos. And thank you Marta, who has provided comfort during my writing, lying quietly with her paw on my foot.

This book would not have happened without my friend and author Dave Dempsey. Dave's thoughtful probing and tidbits of historical information on the Two Hearted watershed sparked my curiosity early on. He has provided a steady encouraging voice over many breakfasts.

Jerry Dennis read an early version of the text, provided organizational and content suggestions, and helped me have confidence that this could be a book. Sharon Flesher, a friend, neighbor, and writer, read an early draft and offered valuable insights. My older sister, Carol, a former English teacher, provided thoughtful and detailed comments. She has been providing input on my writing and proper English my whole life!

In addition, the following folks helped me either as readers or with the various subject matters covered in the book: Brian Beauchamp, Mike Brown, Emily Clegg, Patrick Cotant, Dave Ewert, Ladislov Hanka, BJ Ingwersen, Kristy Jackson, Larry Johnson, Keith King, Bill Knapp, Marlio Lesmez, Keith Magnusson, Sterling McGinn, Mike McTiver, Cathy and Richard Robinson, Tim Scott, Kristie Sitar, and Dave Wiggert. Dave was my graduate advisor at MSU and edited my dissertation in the early 1980s. He reviewed the river flow chapter of this book 40 years later.

Colleen Zanotti met with me to discuss what features to put on a reference map of the Two Hearted watershed. She distilled down a bunch of geographic details and produced an entirely readable map to accompany the text.

After I believed I had a solid draft, the folks at Mission Point Press helped me enter the world of publishing. Doug Weaver and Heather Shaw met with me and described their services and steps in book publishing. Ed Hoogterp reviewed the draft and provided valuable comments and suggestions. Todd Fettig then held my hand and steered me through the publishing process, with help from his team.